"Delightful! Highly entertaining. We all have learned lessons from life, but few possess the ability to share them in such a fun way. Reading this book will make you think some and laugh a lot."

Reg A. Forder
Founder of American Christian Writers

"In *Save Me, I Fell in the Carpool*, Nancy Moser opens the door to her home and her heart to reveal a delightfully warm, humorous, and faith-filled attitude toward life. Nancy endears herself to us all as she humbly admits her missteps as a wife and mother and learns again and again that God forgives and loves us anyway."

Diana L. James
Speaker/Writer and Compiler of
Whatever Happens, You, Too, Can BOUNCE Back

"Nancy Moser fills her stories with words of wisdom. She reminds us that as we provide for our children, God provides for us, and in return he expects our love. Mothers of every age will enjoy these heartwarming stories."

Susan Titus Osborn
Editor, *The Christian Communicator*

Save Me,
I Fell in the Carpool

Nancy Moser

VINE
BOOKS

SERVANT PUBLICATIONS

ANN ARBOR, MICHIGAN

Vine Books is an imprint of Servant Publications especially designed to serve evangelical Christians.

Family and friends have graciously given me permission to use their names and stories in this book.

Published by Servant Publications
P.O. Box 8617
Ann Arbor, Michigan 48107

Cover design: Left Coast Design, Portland, OR
Illustration: Kriege Barrie, Hoquaim, WA

    98 99 00 10 9 8 7 6 5 4 3 2

Printed in the United States of America
ISBN 1-56955-024-7

Library of Congress Cataloging-in-Publicaiton Data

Moser, Nancy.
Save me, I fell in the carpool / Nancy Moser.
    pm.   cm.
ISBN 1-56955-024-7
1. Mothers—Humor.   2. Wives—Humor.   3. Parenting—Humor.
I. Title.
PN6231.M68M66   1998
81805407—dc21   97-35296
                                                CIP

To Mark

For twenty-two years you've kept my head above water.
Don't you *ever* let go.

CONTENTS

Part 3: Relatives and Other Strangers

Part 4: He and Me

PROLOGUE

Save me, O God, for the waters have come up to my neck.
PSALM 69:1

I'm drowning. In the carpool of childhood and the whirlpool of wifedom. I'm floundering in the floodgates of friendship and the muck and mire of motherhood. I often feel I'm up a creek without a paddleboard. The life roles I'm swimming in threaten to pull me under. If only they offered swimming lessons for the sea of life.

What a relief that God doesn't require me to be an expert, that he allows me to wade if I must, do the crawl because it's easy, and even flip over on my back and merely float when I get tired. He doesn't expect me to spring off the starting block, execute a swan dive—or even fit into a swimsuit. He is very patient when I belly flop or get water up my nose.

Yet as I dog paddle through the years trying to keep afloat, I find my head *can* stay above water if I look beyond the torrents that flow around me. If I look up. To God.

Suddenly my arms aren't tired anymore. My legs find new strength to kick and propel myself to the shore. I am safe. My lungs fill with his life-giving breath. My heart settles into the gentle rhythm that proves he is there—and will always be there whether I deserve it or not. He is forever the gentle parent, partner, and protector.

All he asks is that I jump in and get my feet wet. When things are going swimmingly or when life is going down the drain, my job is to remember he's there and to say the three words he longs to hear: "Save me, God."

At that moment he reaches out and pulls me up where I belong. And I am saved.

part 1

K-I-D-S
Is a Four-Letter Word

Having kids is the easy part—taking care of their rumps, grumps, and bumps is the challenge.

Payment Due

I will praise God's name in song
and glorify him with thanksgiving.
This will please the Lord more than an ox,
more than a bull with its horns and hoofs.

PSALM 69:30-31

Going through the labor of childbirth is easy. OK, maybe not easy, but easier than what happens when you get the baby home from the hospital. I don't think any new parent realizes the time that will be involved in taking care of the bun-in-the-oven who's now bigger than a breadbox.

The sacrifices we mothers make during pregnancy—our waistlines, our wardrobes, and our freedom to eat the foods we really love—pale in comparison to the sacrifices we make once the bundle of joy arrives. Every minute of our day is spent focused on this wiggly little being who has no inkling of our sacrifice. If our time is not spent actually touching, talking to, and feeding this new little person, it is spent thinking about, fretting over, and talking *about* him or her.

Our babies are totally helpless—and so are we as we are lured into their world and the spell of their tender existence. We revise our purpose for living to provide, protect, and prepare our children to be all they can be. They cry and we rush to their sides, eager to fulfill their every wish. If they are hungry, we feed them. If they are wet, we change them—or con Grandma into doing it. We give comfort. We wrap them in too many blankets when we venture outdoors. We shackle them into car seats when we drive. And when they start crawling, we follow their every move to protect them from stairs, sharp corners, and the consequences of porcelain knickknacks.

What do we ask in return? We don't ask for monetary consideration. We don't ask for awards or a write-up in the newspaper. We don't even ask for a thank you. All we expect as payment for our loyalty and attention is their love. And we aren't even picky about how it is extended to us. A smile. A laugh. A child's outstretched arms. The indescribable moment as that little head rests against our shoulder. And eventually the most loving words ever spoken: "Mama" and "Dada."

As we provide for our children, God provides for us. He protects and prepares us to be all we can be. And what does he ask from us in return? He doesn't ask for monetary consideration or awards or a write-up in the newspaper. He doesn't even insist on a thank you. All God expects as payment for his loyalty and attention is our love. A smile. A laugh. Our outstretched arms. The indescribable moment as our head bows in surrender and we utter the most loving word ever spoken.

"Lord."

Trade-Offs

But whatever was to my profit I now consider loss for the sake of Christ.

PHILIPPIANS 3:7

We got our youngest daughter, Laurel, by trading in a dog. It's not as bizarre as it sounds.

Laurel was a wanted child. Not that Emily and Carson weren't wanted, planned for, prayed for. They were. But Laurel, our third child, was a bonus, like a sparkly star on homework or a free trial-sized tube of toothpaste with the purchase of a toothbrush.

Having baby number three wasn't an impulsive decision. After having the first two children—and considering we had one of each flavor—we thought we were through having babies. But every once in awhile ...

One day my husband Mark said it out loud. "Let's have another baby."

The thought of it made my stomach contract like it did at the thought of eating liver. And yet the idea was intriguing. Emily would be seven. Carson, four. We had a nice house, good jobs, a big enough car, a dog—

A dog. Forgive me if you are a dog-lover, but I am not. And our dog, Nacho, knew it. From the moment she raced through our front door, that dog slobbered, shed, peed, and chewed on everything—and everyone—just to torment me.

Then the most bizarre thought popped into my head.

"I'll have another baby if we get rid of the dog."

Mark liked Nacho. But he liked me better. So it was agreed. We put an ad in the paper and found a new home for Nacho, thus creating a new home for Laurel. How many children can say they were traded for a dog?

It was a good trade-off, although there have been moments.... At least the baby didn't shed.

Yet we soon discovered that not all trade-offs were so satisfying, though some were more unusual than others. Mark and I had earned an eight-day trip to London through our business. The departure date was March 13. Laurel was due March 2. Even if she were born on time, it would be a challenge. But if she were late ... should we go? Should we stay?

As the due-date approached, I got ready for the trip. With both sets of grandparents in town, we arranged to have the older two kids go with one while the other grandparents got the baby. Halfway through the week, there would be a baby handoff (synchronize your watches, please). The kids would be well cared for, and the grandmas couldn't wait to get their hands on the new baby.

But what about me? Traveling within a few days (who knew how many days) of giving birth ... the physical, the emotional questions. The wardrobe questions (what would I fit into?).

We thought about giving up the trip, but decided against it. We'd always wanted to go to London. And we'd chosen to have this child. The fact that God had arranged for her to be due so close to our departure date complicated, but did not prohibit, our plans.

Luckily, Laurel arrived on time: March 2. Yet once I held her in my arms, I questioned the wisdom of leaving her so soon. She would only be eleven days old. When I took her home from the hospital, I didn't want to let her go. She was in my arms or beside me as many hours of the day as possible. It was as if I wanted to stuff those eight days I'd be missing into the eleven days I had with her. She was the most precious baby. How could I leave her?

It was one of the hardest things I've ever done, walking out that door, getting on that plane. They say the bond between newborn and mother is strong. They're right. If we could bottle it, we'd put Super Glue out of business. It was as if I were emotionally stretched between Laurel and London. A part of me stayed behind. My arms physically ached to hold her.

Looking back, the fact that Laurel and I survived physically and emotionally is truly one of God's miracles. He was merciful. He allowed me to make the trade-off between self-gratification and motherhood. And though I survived—though Laurel survived—I will forever regret leaving her behind. God has forgiven me. Laurel has forgiven me. But as for me forgiving myself....

Some trade-offs are a good deal. Others teach us a lesson.

Don't Drink from the Toilet

God has brought me laughter, and everyone who hears about this will laugh with me.

GENESIS 21:6

T oddlers are amazing people.

Not only do they flourish looking at everyone's knees, they are inventive enough to learn valuable life lessons in spite of it. If only we were so wise....

Lesson Number One: *Don't drink from the toilet.* One of our three children—to protect sensitive pride, I won't reveal which one—discovered that getting a drink of water from the john was easier than asking Mommy to get one from the faucet. "If it's good enough for the cats, it's good enough for me."

When I first discovered this independent youngster, cup dipped in the bowl, sleeve soggy, I was greeted with a toast. "See, Mommy?"

After explaining the finer points of clean water, I silently gave thanks the water in question wasn't ... in use.

Lesson Number Two: *Only Superman can fly.* Toddlers test this rule with great regularity. Beds, ottomans, kitchen counters, stairs, rooftops (delete that last one—I think that was the plot of a recent nightmare). Scaring us to the point of seizure is a toddler's job.

Our eldest, Emily, was the first to get a job-related injury. She hit the bridge of her nose after jumping off the front stoop onto concrete. As the area around her eyes and nose black-and-blued, she looked like a boxer after a hard day at the office.

The admonition, "We don't jump" will go down in the annals of parental history as being one of the weakest pearls of wisdom ever incessantly repeated to no avail. Telling a toddler, "We don't jump" is like telling a politician, "We don't spend." They do, and they do.

Which makes me digress a moment. If I were a toddler, I'd like one question answered: What is this "we" business?

"We need to eat our lima beans."

"We need to take a nap."

"Do *we* have to go potty?"

Any moment now, the toddler population is going to mutiny and demand, "Hey, *you* eat the lima beans, *you* take a nap, and if *you* have to go potty, go! But leave *we* out of it!"

Lesson Number Three: *"Uh-oh" is too late.* This is an early draft of Murphy's Law.

"What happened to the piece of gum I just gave you?"

"Why is there a hole in the box of orange Jell-O?"

"Who put Big Bird in the kitty litter box?"

"How did baby powder get sprinkled on the VCR?"

"Uh-oh."

Lesson Number Four: *Correct pronunciation is optional.* Before children learn to read, they learn the language via the ear. This can lead to some interesting pronunciations and some totally new words. *Grandpa* becomes *Boppa* and *curb* becomes *curve* (Laurel didn't change this last pronunciation until she was eight).

These slight variations on the English language are understandable. However, there were a few words my kids uttered that defied English roots. Latin roots. Martian roots.

When Emily was two, she went through a stage of waking up in the middle of the night. When we'd go in to comfort her, she'd exclaim, "The gape! The gape!" *Ape? Grape? A grape-colored ape?* We never did figure it out, but Emily seemed satisfied when we told her the gape was gone and everything was all right.

Another new word was "hoya." When our oldest two children were little and we'd sit them down to have their picture taken, instead of saying "cheese" Emily used to say "banana" (which led to many odd, open-mouthed portraits). But Carson didn't like that word. He made up his own: *hoya.* As I know for a fact he had not studied botany (still hasn't), I have no knowledge of *hoya's* toddler meaning. I only know that it produced an interesting variation on the open-mouthed "banana" portraits.

Lesson Number Five: *Peaches roll, sandwiches don't.* Laurel discovered this lesson while on a family picnic in front of a mountain lake.

Laurel was doing what we all were doing, sitting on a rock, balancing a sandwich in one hand, a peach in the other, with a sip-it box of juice leaning precariously on the ground close by. But with her pudgy toddler hands, and considering toddlers have no lap to speak of, maneuvering from one bite to the next was the equivalent of accomplishing laser surgery. She had just taken a bite out of her peach and was zoning in on the sandwich. To do so, she had to set the peach down. On the ground. Where it promptly rolled into the lake. She tossed the sandwich and ran after the peach. Only the p.b.& j. was saved, sprinkled liberally with dirt and grass.

Maybe that's another lesson: One can always use more fiber in one's diet.

Now, with my kids past the toddler era, I look back, wiser but wistful. Those few short years were harried, exciting, and exasperating. If only I'd been smart enough to take a deep breath and relish it. There was a life lesson in it for me too: Children are pure joy.

Hoya!

The Gift

This poor widow has put in more than all the others.
All these people gave their gifts out of their wealth;
but she out of her poverty put in all she had to live on.

LUKE 21:3-4

Six children, six years old. Boys. At a birthday party. Excedrin headache #85.

But I was smart. I'd moved the festivities from home sweet home to the local Mexican restaurant that specialized in such things. Why any business would willingly invite gaggles of birthday-crazed children into their establishment to spill drinks, topple chairs, and cover the floor with crumbs was beyond me. But if they were willing, I'd comply—whatever the price. Better their floor than mine.

The Party Coordinator was young (a prerequisite) and enthusiastic (give her time). She herded the boys into a far corner of the restaurant that was marked with balloons tied onto every chair—a warning to other diners: *Stay back! Way back!* As the boys scrambled onto the chairs (knocking two out of the six to the ground) she handed out party hats, including a huge sombrero for Carson, the birthday boy.

I took my camera position a safe distance away, and let her do her stuff.

Pin the tail on the donkey. Bean bag toss. Word scramble (TSROBRUI = BURRITOS). Untied shoelaces, runny noses, bobbing cowlicks.

It was time to open the gifts. The boys sat on their knees and leaned across the table, anxious for Carson to "Open mine first!"

It was then I noticed that one boy, Matthew, was sitting quietly in his chair. He stuffed his hands into the pockets of his down vest. His eyes flitted between Carson and the front door of the restaurant. His legs dangled with a rhythm that quickened with each passing minute.

Paper was ripped. Bows were squashed. One present opened. Two.

Matthew wiggled in his chair. His head jerked toward the door as customers left and others entered. He bit his lip.

What was wrong?

It had something to do with the presents. I counted them. Five guests … four presents.

Matthew didn't have a present to give Carson! I gave an inward sigh. How could I let him know it didn't matter? How could I tell—

Matthew stood. All the presents had been opened—except his.

It's OK, Matthew. You don't need—

Matthew pulled a dog-chewed plastic figure of a soldier out of the pocket of his vest. He handed it to Carson.

"Happy birthday," he said.

I prayed my six-year-old would show some etiquette far beyond his years.

"Thanks, Matthew," Carson said.

Good boy.

"Matthew?"

Matthew's head snapped toward the voice of his mother. She had come in the restaurant unnoticed. She handed him a beautifully wrapped birthday present for Carson.

The look on Matthew's face was worth a hundred gifts. A thousand. His fidgeting stopped. His shoulders straightened as he handed Carson the gift.

"Happy birthday, Carson," he said again.

Carson opened the present.

"Thanks, Matthew," he said. "Thanks for both presents."

Matthew's mother looked puzzled. While the boys were eating their cake and spilling their juice, I let her in on the secret.

I told her about her son's gift of the toy soldier.

Her eyes filled with proud tears. As did mine. We felt honored to have witnessed true giving. From a six-year-old boy. A grimy-faced, scraped-knees, heaven-sent little boy.

A boy who had given all that he had.

When the Feeling's Right

*Pray continually; give thanks in all circum-
stances, for this is God's will for you in Christ
Jesus.*

1 THESSALONIANS 5:17-18

Having kids is emotional. Raising kids is emotional. I guess it's safe to say that the mere thought of the little whipper-snappers is emotional.

Much of our day is spent in the logistics of motherhood: wet bottoms, empty stomachs, and cranky dispositions. When the thought to pray popped into my head, it was handily pushed aside. "Not now, God. I'm busy. Catch you later when I'm in the proper mood."

But with practice, with maturity—and with God's persistence—I learned that he wants us to come to him from wherever we are. From whatever emotion we're feeling.

From sorrow: There were times (are still times) when I felt so overwhelmed that tears were not an option. I'd escape to the baby's room and sit in the rocker, hug a teddy bear to my chest, and bawl. The reasons behind my tears were not earth-shattering. Just a general despair for my lack of time, my lack of parenting skill, my lack of stamina, my inescapable yearning for peanut butter cups in spite of my diet.

"I can't pray now," I'd think. "I'm a mess. I'm acting like a baby myself—"

Pray to me now.

So I did. And he was right.

26

From anger: "Who scribbled in my book?" "Who's been eating the bouillon cubes?" "Who put a golf ball in the microwave?" "Who spilled Kool-Aid on the couch?"

Couldn't I have just one day where there was no crisis? Where things ran like they did in June Cleaver's house? Or Donna Reed's? Or even Jane Jetson's?

"I can't pray now," I'd think. "I'm so mad I feel like throwing the Hamburger Helper against the wall—"

Pray to me now.

So I did. And he was right.

From frustration: Who stole my waist? When would I fit into my clothes again? If I couldn't blame it on a recent pregnancy, what could I blame it on? Who gave the go-ahead to allow those fine lines around my eyes and the permanent crease in my forehead? And my hair … it used to shine. It used to bounce when I walked. Now other things bounce.

I used to be a young woman. Slim. Pretty. Now I'm grim and pouty.

"I can't pray now," I'd think. "I'm vain. I only have complaints. I can't—"

Pray to me now.

So I did. And he was right.

From laughter: I heard the familiar sounds of a Broadway musical coming from the living room. I heard the sounds of jumping. I smiled. I knew what was happening. I snuck a look, not wanting to interrupt the show. Laurel was wearing the purple and magenta dress I'd made for just this purpose: she was singing and dancing to the song "America" from *West Side Story*, which was playing on the VCR beside her. She kicked and spun, trying to match the grace and agility of Rita Moreno and company. She attempted to sing the words which were spouted so fast even I had trouble distinguishing them. Her feet got tangled. She fell. I tried to stifle a laugh but failed. She saw me and put her hands on her hips, challenging me to a dance-duel. I joined her and we danced and sang together. And laughed ...

"I can't pray now," I thought. "It's too silly. We're not being dignified at all—"

Pray to me now.

So I did. And he was right.

From joy: I was lying on the couch, reading. Emily appeared in her nightgown toting *The Secret Garden*.

"Can I?" she asked. I nodded and she took a place at the other end of the couch and opened her book, tucking her feet in her nightgown to keep them warm.

Soon Carson appeared in his Big Bird pj's. He carried a Richard Scarry book, dog-eared from frequent use. I looked up. He raised his eyebrows, letting them ask the question. I nodded and Emily and I pulled our feet in so he could sit on the middle cushion.

I heard the patter of footed pajamas approaching. Laurel appeared with *Pat the Bunny*. She didn't hesitate or bother with a question but climbed on top of me, using my stomach as a chair. The only way I could read my book was to place my arms around her.

We read our books. Cozy, uncomfortable. Together.

"I can't pray now," I thought. "I'm too happy, too content, too—"

Pray to me now.

So I did. He was right.

He's always right. We don't need a special time to pray; a particular setting, a particular emotion. He wants us to call on him from wherever we are, from whatever we are feeling. Any time is the right time to pray.

Pray to me now. So do it. Right now.

Godly by Association

You have made known to me the path of life;
you will fill me with joy in your presence.

ACTS 2:28

Five years ago, Laurel claimed a corner of our basement for playing Barbie. It's out of the main flow of traffic, under a window so there's plenty of light, and next to an antique pedestal table whose legs make interesting outposts for Barbie's exploits. Yet when I used to read to Laurel, we didn't venture into Barbie territory; we sat in the cushy chair in our bedroom. Reading didn't belong in the Barbie corner and nary a Barbie was ever found sitting in the cushy chair. Each place conjured up a specific association and emotion. Kind of like Pavlov's dogs.

It's the same with the chair in front of my computer. As soon as I sit down, my mind fast-forwards to the part of my brain that handles my writing. If I want to read, I move to the living room couch. Yet the same places elicit other states of mind from other people. When the kids sit in my computer chair their minds are ready to play games (and occasionally tackle some homework). When Mark sits on the couch, it's to watch TV. The places we spend our lives spark specific emotions and actions.

This is an amazing phenomenon. Once while going to pick up a takeout pizza, I was trying to work out the intricacies of a plot line for my novel. As I drove the familiar route, the pieces of the plot-puzzle fell into place. I returned home with dinner and ideas. Oddly enough, the next time I went for pizza I tried again with another plot dilemma. And once again, I returned home with dinner and ideas. The mindless drive along familiar streets jump-started my creative process on many occasions (the promise of pepperoni probably helped).

It's not just places. The five senses are steeped in memories and reactions. I have a Christmas sweater. When I put it on, I am transformed by holiday sentiment. When I smell Ivory dish soap I think of my grandma's kitchen in Minnesota. When I taste peanut butter, I think of Eastridge Elementary School. When I hear "Black Water" by the Doobie Brothers I am transported back to a disco on 23rd and "O" Streets where my husband and I did the Hustle in polyester and platform shoes.

It seems everything—every action and every emotion—has its spark. Even God? Certainly we don't have to walk into the sanctuary of a church to tune in to him, or hear the "Hallelujah Chorus" or feel the solid oak of a pew beneath our fanny? Do we?

If we truly love him with all our heart, all our mind, all our soul, and all our strength, we should be thinking about him *all* the time. From the drive to the grocery store to our summer vacation. While we're eating ice cream bars or washing the car. All these mundane moments of our life should be full of thoughts of him.

We have no trouble remembering God during the high points, the big revealing moments that stick in our memories. Often we'd like to linger in those moments, feeling full of him and his presence. But God wants more than that. He wants us to remember him on our way down to normal. In the moments drowning in normal.

The associations that fill up our lives come unbidden. Laurel didn't set out to make the basement corner Barbie territory, and Grandma had no idea I would forever associate Ivory dish soap with her cozy kitchen. Yet the associations that fill our lives with God take a bit more work. As Oswald Chambers says, "It is not done once for always; it is only done *always*."

Think about it. Think about him. Always.

The Reward of Hot Biscuits

Jesus said, "Let the little children come to me,
and do not hinder them, for the kingdom of
heaven belongs to such as these."

MATTHEW 19:14

I love to shop. My kids don't. If asked (don't ask), I'd have to admit that their disdain for the activity is directly related to my love of the activity because I used to drag them along. And I went shopping a lot—with a family of five we always seemed to be in need of milk, shoes, or a birthday present for some school chum.

Taking them along wasn't their choice—or mine either. Mark did his part in the evening and weekends, but during the rest of my free time it was take them or don't go. So they went. Under duress.

We had it down to a military maneuver. *All right men, take your positions!* At stores with carts, Emily ducked under the basket, Carson got inside, and Laurel in the seat. With the combined weight of the kids and my purchases (tucked around, on top of, and under Carson) it was like pushing a wagon train uphill—especially when Emily dragged her feet.

In stores without carts the kids scrambled behind me, our hands forming a chain as if we were ready to play Red Rover or Crack the Whip. My eyes would scope out a safe place to park them while I shopped nearby, usually in a corner near a three-way mirror where they could smear someone else's glass with their fingerprints and multiply their images so it appeared I was shopping with a legion of kids—a terrifying thought. Besides the fascination of the mirror, the kids were armed with books, dolls, Transformers, and Cheerios. Most of the time they stayed put but if I'd temporarily misplace one of them, that one would invariably pop out from the middle of a circular rack, delighted to scare me. I'm sure the clerks found our visits taxing as, in addition to the fingerprints, we'd leave behind racks of slightly rumpled clothes and a trail of smashed cereal rings—proof that the Moser gang had passed through.

If I felt like testing the limits of endurance, I took the time to try on clothes. The four of us would cram into a dressing room where the kids would sit at my feet. Carson would dutifully close his eyes on command and then they would advise me as to whether it looked "pretty" or "icky." They were usually right. However, due to the limits of our sanity, most of the time I bought first, tried on at home, and returned the icky ones … which gave me another chance to venture out with the troops.

The kids had favorite stores and not-so-favorite stores. Their favorite had a play land with an elephant they could climb on before sliding out its trunk. I'd feel safe leaving them there if I were close by—a decision I cringe at now. But the search for a few moments of solitary shopping often leads a mother to do stupid things.

As for their least favorite stores … at sixteen, Carson still cringes when we pass his least favorite. "I hate that place," he says. "You used to take *so* long." No doubt, he's scarred for life and some future daughter-in-law will hate me for creating a damaged shopping psyche.

Yet there were rewards to our shopping expeditions. Afterward, if they'd been good—and if I didn't have a headache, I considered them good—we stopped and got hot buttermilk biscuits. An earthly reward that tasted of heaven.

All in all, our expeditions were usually successful. No one ever got truly lost—proof that there is safety in numbers and loud voices. If during head count I'd find only two out of the three, I'd only have to ask, "Where'd they go?" and I'd immediately receive the satisfaction of a sibling's vindictive finger, "Thataway" (usually toward the nearest toy department).

I can't imagine the panic Joseph and Mary must have felt when they discovered—after a day's travel away from Jerusalem—that Jesus was missing. His absence was hardly the same as a short detour to the toy department. They rushed back to the city. Yet it still took them three more days to find him in the temple, speaking to the elders. Somehow it's comforting that their reaction is our reaction: "Son, why have you treated us like this? Your father and I have been anxiously searching for you" (Luke 2:48). I love a subsequent verse: "Then he went down to Nazareth with them and was obedient to them" (verse 51). What a good kid.

Just like my kids. They stray and they obey. And I worry and I pray. And we share some moments of our day. Together. The reward of that is better than hot biscuits.

Tuning In

Let the wise listen and add to their learning,
and let the discerning get guidance.

"**G**a!"

My mother pounced on the word. "Come quick! Emily said 'Grandma!'"

I finished mixing Emily's rice cereal with some formula.

"Nancy! Come in here! She said it!"

I dutifully went into the living room to hear proof that my firstborn was a prodigy. Mom had Emily seated in her infant seat and was cajoling her with animated facial expressions.

"Come on, sweetie," she said. "You can do it. Say 'Grandma.'"

I tucked a bib under Emily's chin. "Mom, she's too little. She can't say 'grandma.'"

"Maybe not all of it, but she—"

"So she said part of it?" I asked. "As in 'gram'?"

"Not exactly."

"'Gam'?"

"Not exactly."

"I'm running out of letters," I said.

Mom looked at me disgustedly. "She said 'ga.' She looked right at me and said 'ga.' And she smiled."

Actually, Emily was probably saying, "Golly gee, won't this lady ever leave me alone?"

"She says 'phfkjz' too," I said. "If you can tell me what that means, I'll get you a job with the United Nations."

My mother squared her shoulders and proceeded to feed Emily. "You don't have to believe me," she said. "But Emily and I know what she said."

It's odd how we are so eager for our kids to talk. We don't realize we're going to spend the rest of their childhoods telling them "Shh!" The key is: if we teach them how to talk, we have to teach them how to be quiet. I taught Emily this rule when she was five years old and we were riding in the car. I can remember the exact intersection where it happened....

Emily was rambling on—and on—about kindergarten, what she wanted to be for Halloween, the offenses of her two-year-old brother, Carson, and wondering if we called autumn "fall" because the leaves fell off the trees. Yet when Emily asked questions, she didn't pause long enough for me to answer. She was already zipping on to another subject. It was not a discussion. It was a monologue. It was exhausting keeping up with the workings of her little mind. It soon became apparent that whatever popped into her head popped out of her mouth. To be truthful, since she wasn't concerned with my involvement (and since it would have been difficult to get a word in anyway), while she rambled, I visited my own mental list of errands, schedules, and—

There was a moment of silence. Its sudden existence was shocking. I looked at Emily. She looked at me, her forehead furrowed.

"What's wrong?" I asked.

She sighed deeply. "I can't keep talking all the time. It makes me tired."

What? "You don't *have* to talk all the time," I said.

"I *don't?*"

I shook my head. "We can ride without saying a word," I

said hopefully. "Or you can listen."

"To what?"

"To me. To what's going on outside. To what's going on inside. To the air rushing by."

"Wow," she said. "I'm so glad."

I have no idea where Emily got the notion she was expected to keep the air filled with words. I'm a talkative person, but even I take a breath once in awhile and I actually enjoy extended moments of silence. There are times to talk and times to—

Emily's misconception made me wonder how many times we think we have to talk *at* God in a never-ending banter. Do we wait for the answers to our questions? If we're not interested in his involvement—if we make it too hard for him to get a word in—he might just tune us out. We need to remember Emily's lesson: We don't need to talk all the time.

Sometimes, we need to listen. To each other. To what's going on outside. To what's going on inside. To the air rushing by.

Who knows? The air may be full of God's whispering voice, calling our name. Or maybe just telling us "Shh."

Home of the Whopper

This is the confidence we have in approaching God: that if we ask anything according to his will, he hears us.

1 John 5:14

"And I want a chocolate cake with pink frosting and red juice and chocolate-chip ice cream and—"

I put up a hand, stopping Laurel's monologue. "I know exactly what you want, sweetie. Down to the last jelly bean."

"Jelly beans!" she said. "I forgot about the jelly beans on top of the cake. I want pink ones and red ones—no black ones at all, save those for Dad—and purple ones and—"

"Let me handle it. I said I'd give you a whopper of a birthday party and I meant it. But you're taking all the fun out of it by telling me how to do it."

"I just want to make sure it's done right," Laurel said. "I want you to know exactly—"

"I know all about your 'exactlys.'" I pulled her under my arm for a hug. "I know you. I know everything you like. I know what makes you happy. I can go into a store full of a thousand dolls and pick the one you'd like the best."

"The one with the fanciest dress."

I nodded. "I can go to the cookie aisle at the grocery store and never miss."

"Oreos," we said together.

"So relax," I said. "Trust me. I'll give you a birthday party you'll never forget."

She left me alone to plan the party. I got out a note pad and settled into the blue chair by the fireplace.

"What's the theme? We have to have a theme," I mumbled to myself. "Laurel's birthday is close to Easter this year...." I shot up straight. "Rabbits. We can have a rabbit theme!" I started scribbling notes.

I wish Laurel would trust me.

"The girls can make rabbits out of Styrofoam balls ..."

Doesn't she realize I know her innermost dreams?

"... they can have hats and wiggly eyes...."

When she keeps bugging me about how she wants it done, it hurts my feelings.

"We'll get bunny-shaped plastic boxes and fill them with candy."

She takes some of the joy away when she doesn't leave me alone to give freely.

"I'll get pastel-colored plates and napkins and have balloons to match...."

Doesn't she know I'd give her the world if she'd let me? ... I wish someone knew my deepest dreams. I wish someone would offer me my greatest desires—

I stopped writing. Oh, dear.

Someone did know my deepest dreams. Someone did offer me my greatest desires.

God.

Had I been like Laurel, directing God, putting in my two cents instead of trusting him? Was he reluctant to fulfill my dreams until I showed him that I believed in him completely?

I put the note pad aside and bowed my head. I revamped my prayers—the ones I pestered God with on a regular basis. I gave him my heart's desire and said, "Take care of it, please."

Fear grabbed hold of my insides. What if he didn't want to give me my dream? What if it wasn't in his plan? Was this fear the reason I kept badgering him with the details of how *I* wanted my prayers to be answered (just like Laurel kept after me with mentions of chocolate cake and jelly beans)?

I took a deep breath. I calmed my breathing. I forced the fear to let go. My next prayer was hard.

"Whatever you want to happen is fine with me, Lord. Even if you choose to close the door on my dream, I know you'll open a window."

I sat back, feeling satisfied. Content. Now that I was letting God plan the party of my life, I knew he'd create a whopper.

I can hardly wait.

The Reward of Being Lazy

*Whoever watches the wind will not plant; who-
ever looks at the clouds will not reap.*

ECCLESIASTES 11:4

"But I don't want to set the table." Eight-year-old Laurel flung herself onto the couch in the den where I was dusting. She drew a melodramatic hand across her brow. "I have a headache," she moaned.

We were used to Laurel's diversions. She had a tendency to contract mysterious ailments when work threatened. Her arm hurt ... or a leg ... or a finger.

"The table's not going to set itself," I said.

There was a moment's hesitation. "I wish I were a cat," she said, playing conversational hopscotch.

"Why?"

"Look at them."

I stopped my dusting and looked toward the window where Pepper and Lucy were draped in the sun.

"They never have to do chores. They never have to do homework or match up their socks or eat the mushrooms on their pizza."

"You do have a rough life."

Laurel nodded and sighed. Pepper and Lucy must have realized we were talking about them because they opened one eye each, twitched an ear, and rolled over to let their backsides bake in the sun.

I finished dusting a bookshelf and moved to the desk.

"Lying around being lazy all day would be nice for awhile," I said. "But I bet it would get boring, pretty fast."

Laurel shook her head. "It would be fun."

"I don't think so," I said. "The kitties' lives are the same day after day. There are no rewards for doing a good job. No high points. No bikes to ride. No Monopoly marathons. No making cookies with Grandma. No getting an 'A' on a spelling test of the fifty states."

"No low points either," said Laurel. "No boys trying to make me laugh during reading. No skinned knees when I rollerblade. No crying when Beth dies in *Little Women*."

"You're right," I said. "There'd be no crying."

Laurel fingered her lower lip, thinking hard. "But no laughing either. Like when Dad sings 'Viva Las Vegas.'"

I chuckled at the mere thought of it. "No laughing, either."

Laurel moved to the sunshine and sprawled between the cats, stroking Lucy's black fur. "I suppose I would miss those things if all I did was sit in the sun and be lazy."

I looked at Laurel. At the cats. On a whim I put down my dust cloth.

"Move over," I said.

Laurel edged closer to Lucy while Pepper gave me a questioning glance. I stretched out on my stomach and looked out the window. The breeze made the leaves flutter. A bird soared. The sun warmed my face. This wasn't too bad. Not bad at—

It didn't take long for Pepper to decide four was a crowd. She stood and arched her back, stretching her front paws until they quivered. "See?" I said, remembering the lesson I was trying to teach. "Even Pepper knows there's a time to move on."

"If you mean it's time to set the table—"

"I mean it's time," I said.

I stood and held out my hand to help Laurel up. She took it and groaned as if her muscles were as old as mine.

"Tell you what," I said. "You set the table and I'll finish dusting. Then we'll meet back here in ten minutes."

"To lie in the sun?" Her eyes narrowed, giving me the *gotcha* look children give when they think they've caught their parents being illogically human. "Won't that be acting lazy?" she said.

I tweaked her nose. "As long as your work's done, being lazy can be one of life's high points."

And it was.

Carpooling Without a Life Jacket

All that the Father gives me will come to me, and whoever comes to me I will never drive away.

JOHN 6:37

Please note these simple safety rules of life: don't put marbles up your nose, don't gesture with a fork while you're talking, and wear a life jacket when you jump or are pushed into the carpool.

Our family is fortunate. We live close enough to school so the kids walk or ride their bikes. Unless water is involved. Rain, sleet, snow—or the imminent threat thereof. Precipitation heralds the beginning of telephone negotiations worthy of any diplomat. Laurel calls her best friend, Rae Chelle, and they try to remember whose turn it is to drive. Since mothers are only consulted as a last resort, the conversation usually goes something like this:

"Mom? Can you drive us to school?"

"Didn't I drive last Wednesday when it rained?"

"You drove *to* but Rae Chelle's mom picked up *after*. Can you do it again 'cause Rae Chelle's mom has a doctor's appointment and her little brother's sick and they ran out of Rice Krispies so they're running late and she can't after."

"So am I taking or picking up?"

A pause. "Let me check."

I realize it would be easier to speak directly to Rae Chelle's mom but I don't because there's a rule that says weekday mornings aren't supposed to be easy. So I do my part.

Because I work at home, I don't bother dressing up to do my carpool duty. In fact, I feel downright chic if I put on shoes. To shoe or not to shoe is determined in the final moments as I grab my keys. If I feel brave, I scurry to the car shoeless and pray that I don't run out of gas, get rear-ended, or meet up with my own mother—who supposedly taught me common sense.

Remember that scene from *Mr. Mom* where Michael Keaton gets scolded for going the wrong way through the carpool lane at school? It's true, all true. The way the elementary school has its carpool routine laid out is as complicated as a gold-medal figure skating program—the long program. By the time I escape back into street traffic I figure I've done a double axel, a flying camel, and a sit spin. If it's a good day, the judges give me a 5.9 for my technical ability and a perfect 6.0 for my dazzling carpool artistry.

Our carpool usually includes food and drink. Part of it's my fault. I'm rarely seen without my trusty can of Diet Coke—inevitably bringing chants of "Don't drink and drive, Mrs. Moser" from the carpoolees. Smart-alecky kids. The rest of the problem I blame on those handy cup-holders that cars and minivans have these days. Talk about an invitation. After a trip through Carpool Land those cup-holders are full of jelly beans, used gum, crumpled Dorito bags, and assorted ponytail bands—all of which are permanently adhered to the holder with the greatest glue ever invented: dried apple juice.

If you have a keen interest in colds and allergies, you'll feel right at home in a carpool. It seems the only tissues ever found in a child's possession are those shredded and fossilized in their pockets after making the washer-dryer rounds. *If* a child does have a fresh tissue, it is of no use as it is buried beneath layers of jackets, backpacks, and science projects.

A nose is running. A sneeze is bursting. A cough is hacking. What's a poor child to do? I have a box of tissues in the car, just for the occasion. But what happens to the tissue when it's served its purpose? Since their pockets are already full of the day's earlier treasures (just waiting to be fossilized), the kids stuff the used tissues in between the seats or in a cup-holder—if they can find one miraculously empty. Or they give it to the baby to chew on.

Carpooling demands iron nerves, deaf ears, and eyes in the back of your head. If you somehow avoid drowning in the deep end of the carpool you'll deliver all the kids to the correct locations and make it back home yourself (if, after all this, you still remember where you live).

When you get there, shut the garage door on the world, toss your keys on the counter, and try a different pool—one that steams and makes your skin pucker. Calgon, take me away.

The Goody Bag

Bear with each other and forgive whatever griev-
ances you may have against one another. Forgive
as the Lord forgave you.

COLOSSIANS 3:13

The Spanish Inquisition missed a verified form of torture: traveling eleven hours in a car with three children. A parent will betray his or her country—or at least blurt out the secret family recipe for Chili Con Carne—at the mere mention of traveling out of town with a carload of ... them.

Remember *them?* Those glorious beings you gave up caffeine for, labored with, and patted baby powder on? Those beings whose switch is stuck in the ON position during the early morning hours when the only programs on TV are half-hour commercials for weight loss products and wrinkle cream? Those beings who stick their fingers through the Life Saver, in the mashed potatoes, and up their noses?

On good days we feel lucky to know *them* and on bad days we consider trading *them* in for a Beta VCR or a salad shooter.

Don't feel guilty. We're talking survival here. Especially when a vehicle is involved.

The seat belts are fastened. The door locks click into place. I shudder. We're trapped—trapped in a space smaller than a bathroom but without the essential facilities. A space that has no potty chair, no refrigerator, and no way to show the tapes of *101 Dalmatians* and *Bambi*. My throat is dry. *I* have to go to the bathroom. I notice my husband crossing himself (and we're not even Catholic). I realize it's going to take a heavy-duty miracle to keep him from pulling into the nearest Holiday Inn and calling it a vacation—even though it's only three blocks from home. It's going to take . . .

The Goody Bag.

The Goody Bag came into existence on an eleven-hour trip to Colorado. It was my secret weapon—a secret I hoarded until the last possible minute. Unfortunately, that minute occurred only sixty minutes away from home.

"He looked at me."

"Hungry, Mama."

"I want to go home."

I turned toward the backseat and grinned at them, knowing sanity was close at hand.

"Who'd like a surprise?" I asked.

Dumb question.

Out came the Goody Bag. Setting it on my lap and opening it only wide enough for me to peek inside (showmanship is essential here), I whipped out three coloring books and three boxes of crayons. Out came the lap desks. Down went the decibel level.

"What's that I *don't* hear?" Mark asked.

"Shh," I said, closing my eyes for a quick nap. "You'll jinx it."

I'd be lying if I said I got to sleep. Let's just say my brain had a brief visit to the Land of Neutral. Pure bliss. For twenty minutes.

"What else do you have in the bag, Mom?"

"More, peez."

"Is there candy in there?"

It was time to play my trump card. "You'll get your next treat from the Goody Bag in one hour—if you're good."

How lucky we are to have raised three angelic children. Nary a pulled hair, pinched arm, or tattling tale in sight.

Hour after hour, the Goody Bag was purged: finger puppets, packages of cheese and crackers, stickers, doll clothes, fancy pencils, markers, pads of paper, tape stories, juice boxes, trolls, books ...

I'd like to say all went smoothly, but you'd know I was lying. Actually, the Goody Bag remained closed after Hour Five because someone (I won't name names) thought it would be neat to draw on the back of Dad's seat. But I guarantee you, by Hour Six, they were angels again.

Our kids are nineteen, sixteen, and twelve now—far too old for the Goody Bag. Wrong. The first year I tried to dispense with it, they pounced on me before we got out the door.

"Where's the Goody Bag?" they asked.

"You're too old for the—"

"No, we're not!" they whined (they've got it down to a perfectly tuned three-part chorus).

While they waited in the car, I scoured the house for appropriate Goody Bag essentials—which had changed a bit through the years. Playing cards, magazines, football cards, markers, cassettes. And those little packages of cheese and crackers—they never outgrow those.

Odd how the lure of the Goody Bag has the same power now as it did then. The Spanish Inquisition will have to think of another torture. In our house, the Goody Bag reigns triumphant.

Waiting Too Long

But they all alike began to make excuses.

LUKE 14:18

My ten-year-old's room was a mess.

No great revelation there. I knew it was a mess. She knew it was a mess. *But* she didn't know I knew it was a mess. The situation would have made a grand Abbott and Costello skit.

One afternoon I was seized with an absurd urge to help Laurel clean it. After taking two aspirins to cure this bizarre symptom only to have it doggedly hang on, I announced my intentions.

"I'm going to help you clean your room."

Stunned silence. Then, "You don't have to do that, Mom. It's not that bad." (This was tantamount to saying the destruction after a tornado is "not that bad.")

I gave her a look that implied I knew how far the truth was being stretched. I also gave her a way out. "I'll give you fifteen minutes to pick it up before I come in and help you really clean—the drawers, your closet—"

"Fifteen minutes?"

I knew she'd prefer fifteen years, but even I wasn't *that* tolerant. "Fifteen minutes," I said. I checked my watch. "Starting now."

Laurel ran up the stairs as if I'd shot off a starting pistol. As I heard construction going on overhead I questioned the wisdom of giving her a head start in cutting a swath across her floor by transferring everything into the drawers and closet that I was about to clean. But my motives were twofold: I wanted her to save face and I didn't want to get angry. If only kids knew how reluctant we parents are about getting angry. If there were some way to avoid that emotion altogether, I'd make a million dollars on the talk-show circuit.

Fourteen minutes into the fifteen, she reappeared.

"All ready for me?" I asked.

She burst into tears. "I need more time."

"How much 'more time'?"

She sniffed loudly. "Forever. It's messier than picking up will fix. I waited too long."

Finally. A true confession.

I headed for the stairs. Laurel ran after me as if she were saving me from ascending the steps to the north tower of the Bastille—and *her* doom. Halfway up the stairs I stopped and faced her, bracing myself for the sight ahead. "Why did you wait so long?" I asked.

Why did you wait so long?

I didn't hear her rambling excuses. I was too busy listening to my own. Why did I wait so long to excavate the refrigerator, balance the checkbook, organize my desk, call a friend, read a book, write letters, study the Bible, get closer to God ...

I was as guilty as Laurel at putting off the should-do's of my life. Her excuses were similar to mine. Priorities skewed, easier pleasures taken first.

It was so easy putting things off as if time were indefinite and available at my convenience. *I'll do it tomorrow. Next week. Next—*

All should-do's were not created equal. Friends, letters, even the checkbook demanded attention. The desk and refrigerator could be stacked higher with a little ingenuity. But other should-do's had more serious consequences....

Had I been putting off God? The consequences of missing a chance to know him better were far-reaching. Eternal. The moments spent with him *had* to come first. And the rest of my life—the humdrum moments that comprised the bulk of my days—would no doubt run smoother if I made room for him by my side. He was waiting for me to bring him front and center.

But had I waited too long? In Laurel's words, was my life messier than picking up would fix?

"Mom?"

I realized I was standing on the stair.

"Aren't you going to help me with my room?"

"Of course—"

She took my hand as we neared the door. "I know I've done wrong and I'll try to do better," she said.

Dear God, I know I've done wrong and I'll try to do better.

I entered her room. Definitely post-tornado.

"Don't be mad," she said, as I opened (or tried to open) a jumbled drawer.

I took a deep breath and dug in for some hard work. How could I be angry with Laurel? Because of her messy room I'd realized my own "room" was a mess. Both could be cleaned up and organized if we got our priorities straight.

And didn't wait too long.

When No One's Watching

*I guide you in the way of wisdom
and lead you along straight paths.
When you walk, your steps will not be hampered;
when you run, you will not stumble.*

PROVERBS 4:11-12

"Look, Mom. Someone got pulled over."

The swirling lights of a police car signaled a job well done.

"They were speeding, weren't they?" Laurel said.

I made a quick glance at my own speedometer. Thirty-nine mph in a thirty-five zone. I lifted my foot from the accelerator and let the car ease down to the legal limit.

"I feel sorry for them," Laurel said, craning her head to watch the police officer write the ticket as we drove past.

I was less obvious, but no less curious. *There, but for the grace of God, go I....*

"Do you ever speed, Mom?"

Oh, boy.

Luckily she didn't wait for my answer.

"Have you ever gotten a speeding ticket?"

That one was easier.

"No, I haven't," I said, truthfully.

But how many times had I willingly bent the law when I thought there was a good chance I wouldn't get caught?

"I see the police cars hiding sometimes," Laurel said. "They sit on the side of the road or in driveways. It's like they're setting a trap for people."

There are a lot of traps in life....

54

"They're just doing their job," I said. Reminding myself. Warning myself.

"It would be nice if everybody followed the rules even when no one was watching," said my wise little Laurel.

"Doing the right thing even when you don't have to." I said. "That's a true test of character."

Laurel turned her attention forward again and readjusted her seat belt. "Like when the teacher leaves the room you shouldn't scream."

I had to laugh. I imagined a primal yelp emanating from elementary school rooms as the poor teachers momentarily left the little darlings on their own.

"Scream?" I asked.

"Well, maybe not scream. Get rowdy. Talk loud."

I nodded. I understood completely. How easy it was to adjust the rules toward our own ends when no one was watching.

Putting your feet up on the desk when the boss wasn't around.

Parking in a handicapped space because you'll only be a minute.

Shoving your empty shopping cart aside instead of taking the time to put it in the cart corral of the parking lot.

And driving above the speed limit when no one's watching.

"God's always watching us, isn't he, Mom?"

I checked the speedometer one more time. Thirty-five. I was doing OK. For the moment. But I knew I could do better—in a lot of ways. For the Big Boss. Just because it was the right thing to do.

"You bet he's watching."

She looked at me and smiled. "Then we'd better not scream."

With wonderful restraint we held it in.

God would be so proud.

Is It Your Birthday Again?

As you know, we consider blessed those who have persevered.

Birthdays come too often.

I'm not complaining about my own birthday coming once a year. Although it is annoying that I can't be thirty-five forever, I have accepted my own milestone (or millstone) as inevitable. My complaint refers to my children's birthdays.

The problem started when I timed my pregnancies with the weather in mind. I decided I wanted to be pregnant during the winter months—mostly because the thought of wearing a maternity swimsuit gave me hives.

Remember the saying, "Be careful what you wish for, it may come true"? Bingo. All three of my children were born within thirty calendar days of each other: March 2, March 21, and April 1. There were a few years in between, but the effect was the same.

Every year, I have to plan—and execute—three birthday parties in thirty days.

When they were little, I cheated. I asked the grandparents over at some compromised date and served one cake with two or three names on it. Happy Birthday. Happy Birthday. Happy Birthday.

My oldest child, Emily, was the first to complain. She didn't think it was fair that she, an old woman of eight, had to share a birthday party with her five-year-old brother and one-year-old

56

sister. Picky kid. I admit it was hard finding a motif that incorporated Barbie, Legos, *and* Miss Piggy.

So I listened to my daughter—in itself a novel idea. The following year I explored the concept of three separate celebrations. Turns out every place from McDonald's to the local gymnastics school had a birthday party plan. I could spend from $1.50 a child to an amount that would require a second mortgage. A party director (job requirements: nerves of steel and no children of his or her own) would serve the little angels cake and lead them in a few party games. All I had to do was take pictures and load the presents into the car—after paying the bill. ("Please, come again.")

I succumbed. We Chuck E Cheesed, Burger Kinged, and Amigoed enough years to make me a stockholder by default. March became an expensive month, second only to December.

When they got older, I realized it was time to be more creative. The year the kids turned sixteen, thirteen, and nine, we tried three different routes, thus making me yearn for the good old days of restaurant parties.

Emily had a "Tell Me When It's Morning" party: your basic slumber party nightmare. The key was overkill. In order to assure the teenyboppers remained in their cage (the basement), I supplied them with a night's worth of wholesome videos (two dozen), ten thousand calories of junk food (nothing red, it stains the carpet), and one telephone. I also purchased a set of ear plugs—for me. I closed the basement door and asked God to grant me patience and Emily a hefty dose of self-control. In the morning—having heard that post-party rubble is the leading cause of heart attacks in parents under the age of fifty—I did not venture into the basement before Emily hosed it down and removed all evidence of … whatever it was they did.

Carson celebrated with a "See You Later" party. A good choice. Although it was expensive, the advantages of the See You Later party far outweighed the extra bucks. I drove Carson and a few of his friends to the nearest theater, where I dropped them off. They saw a movie and stuffed themselves with enough popcorn, Kit Kats, and nachos to make their pubescent faces greasy for a week.

Warning: do not go to the movie with them. This point is critical, as all adolescents, especially those traveling in birthday gaggles, will sit in the front row of the theater and talk, squirm, and visit the restroom at least forty-seven times during the two-hour movie. To ignore this warning is to risk temporary insanity—and a stiff neck.

I gave Laurel a "Wearing a Dress Won't Kill You" party. When we stipulated on the invitation that the girls should wear their Sunday best, every mother called.

"Are you serious?" they asked.

You'd think I'd asked their daughters to wear an ermine robe and a tiara. In an age of sweat pants and T-shirts, dressing up for a party is as foreign as wearing a hat on Easter. But after the initial shock, I got another reaction.

"I remember dressing up for parties," they said. "It was kind of fun."

Imagine that.

When Mark saw me getting out the best china and crystal, he grabbed Carson and escaped before our civility infected the male species. We played every bridal shower game I could think of: Scrambled Words, Memory Tray, and Guess the Advertiser. Cake was eaten amid giggles and raised pinkies. At the end of the two hours, I was tired but wiser. I'd made an amazing discovery: you are what you wear. (I peer down at the clothes I'm wearing as I write this, and I cringe at the implication.) The little girls—for a few hours at least—were proper young ladies.

Soon there will only be two birthday parties and then, only one. Will I feel sad when my party-coordinator days are over?

Nah. By then I'll have grandchildren. I only hope their birthdays fall in the other eleven months of the year. March 2 through April 1 will remain booked—at least in my memories.

School's Out and Other Tortures

"To what can I compare this generation?"
MATTHEW 11:16

"School's out!"

My three children toss their backpacks in the entry closet (where they take root until September), flip off their shoes (making matching scuffs on the wall), and grab the cats in a celebratory hug (the cats slither away).

"Mom? Are you OK?" they ask, noticing my skin matches the ecru of the walls.

A shiver runs from my headband down to the cuffs of my sweat pants. I notice the kitties cowering under the hutch and consider joining them.

"I'll be all right," I say out loud. *"In September,"* I add to myself.

The kids run off to do whatever it is they do when they have nothing to do.

I shuffle into my office and close the door. I sit in the chair in front of my computer. I stare at the page on the screen that was suspended when I heard the first fateful slam of the door.

They're back.

Before I start to whine, let me state that I love my kids. I realize they are a special gift from God. But that doesn't mean I can't cringe at the sound of their elephantine feet on the stairs, or shudder at the mess in the kitchen when they decide to make one humongous chocolate chip-coconut-raisin-oatmeal cookie (which never does cook all the way through). And when the sweethearts file into my office every hour, on the hour, to ask "What can we do now?" I allow myself a flinch.

It's a little-known fact that summer vacation originated in the torture chambers of dark, dank castles but was deemed too harsh. It was put on hold for hundreds of years only to be reinstated as the bane of the twentieth century. Now that I'm an adult, and no longer a recipient of the blessings of my own reprieve from school, I can state unequivocally: it's not fair.

Luckily (this may be a poor choice of adverbs), I work at home. And though I suffer through the pitfalls of having the kids underfoot during the quiet times I normally write, I truly pity those parents who work outside the home. They get a double whammy because they have to find (and pay for) day care for their school-age children who are usually suitably entertained and educated during the working hours of the day. Or worse, if the kids are old enough to stay at home by themselves while their parents are at work, the parents lose all productivity (except in producing an ulcer) by wondering—and worrying— what their kids are doing at home. Alone.

I *know* what they're doing.

They're leaving the door open. Their reason comes right out of *Goldilocks and the Three Bears*: "It's too hot" or "It's too cold." Either way, it creates an air-conditioning bill that rivals the grocery bill. A flurry of mosquitoes and flies is a special bonus.

They're eating. A lot. How I long for school lunches … hot, nutritious food at a reasonable price. With the kids home I bid my own personal favorites adieu: popcorn, V-8, and a Snickers bar I had hidden behind the canned spinach (now *that* is a safe place). In the summer I have to plan five additional meals a week. Meals that contain vitamins.

On the other side of the menu are the children of two working parents. Home alone with no parent to guide them toward the handy standbys of p.b.& j., Fritos, and an apple, they tend to graze, wiping out the pantry quicker than a herd of Mary's little lambs.

They're bringing in interlopers, a.k.a.: the neighbor kids. Some parents say they don't mind having the neighbor kids over to play because it's a way of knowing where their own children are. Baloney. As July fades into August, let the kids make a tent-city of sheets in someone else's living room. Let them finger-paint on someone else's kitchen table—and floor. Let them play beauty parlor with someone else's make-up. Hey, I'm willing to share.

They're getting bored. After a few weeks, I use up all my good responses to their wails of boredom. I start to digress. "The garage needs cleaning," "The house needs painting," "The nation's budget needs balancing." They finally stop asking.

When the end of summer glows on the horizon and the aura of back-to-school entices, I realize there will come a time when I'd give anything to hear the bass-beat of Petra or Jars of Clay at nine o'clock in the morning, and glory to the smell of chlorine-encrusted towels. I'll look back on these chaotic summers with a bittersweet reflection. Guilt will sit on my shoulders until I admit my insensitivity.

But then again, maybe not. I'll work on it.

part 2

Teens:
An Aptitude for Attitude

"I know!" is their anthem.
"Oh, no you don't!" is our descant.

Being Human

Stand firm and hold to the teachings we passed on to you.

2 THESSALONIANS 2:15

If you want to teach something, be something.

Sounds good.

Sometimes I wish I could tell my kids to carry on, do what they know is right, and don't mind me. Being a hypocrite is easy. Being a role model takes work—more work than I'm up to, as I'm tethered and weathered by the moments of life.

When my three children were small, I could get away with the convenience of, "Do as I say, not as I do." They didn't notice the Milky Way wrapper on the counter as I made dinner. They didn't say a word when I wore socks with holes in the toes, and they were too busy playing with Kermit the Frog and Candy Land to see me clean the entry floor after tracking in my own share of mud. Or perhaps they were too much in awe of Mommy to say anything.

Maybe not.

But as they graduated to Barbie, Battleship, and beyond, their minds grasped a scary new concept—independent thought. That's when they began to challenge me and my two-faced behavior.

"How come we have to make our beds when your bed isn't made yet?"

"Uh, I don't know."

"How come we can only watch TV an hour a night and you can watch more?"

"Uh, I don't know."

"How come your coat is hanging on the back of a chair and ours have to be hung up?"

"*Uh, I don't*—" I shake my head, stalling until I conjure up a desperate parent's jewel: "Because I'm the mom, that's why!"

They roll their eyes and leave me to my humiliation. How'd they get so smart? Certainly it wasn't by my example.

It doesn't help my self-esteem to remember my own mother's perfection. I never caught her in a *faux pas*. No wet towels on the floor, no crumbs brushed onto the kitchen floor, no televisions blaring at a ridiculous level (can I help it if I like to *feel* my movies?). She taught us by example. When she worked till the early morning hours sewing a prom dress, we learned to be industrious. When she made the roast and leftover corn last for two more meals, we learned to be thrifty. When she made quilts for the less fortunate, we learned to be charitable.

What am I teaching my kids?

There are *some* good things. When I get an article rejected but send it out again and again until it finally sells, they learn persistence. When I hug their father right in front of them and even give him a kiss (gasp!) they learn love. When I tell them how a prayer was answered, they learn faith.

Not too bad.

Although I *am* working on making my bed, limiting my television time, and hanging up my coat, above all—flaws and all—I'm teaching my children that we're in this together. I don't know all the answers, although I do know a bit more than they do. I have good traits I hope they'll embrace and bad habits I hope they'll avoid.

They know I'm not perfect.

If you want to teach something, be something.

I'm human. Human I can teach. Human I can be.

Perhaps, somehow, they'll learn from that.

The Wallet of Wisdom

The mouth of the righteous man utters wisdom,
and his tongue speaks what is just.

PSALM 37:30

Our son is smart. Brilliant. A genius.

Now that you're done rolling your eyes, let me explain. I'm not speaking of the 2+2=4 kind of smart (though Carson does have his moments). I'm speaking of the wisdom that pops from the mouths of our children unsolicited and unannounced. The wisdom that makes us grownups feel the need to … grow up.

It all started at a basketball game. The winter holidays were neatly tucked away until next year. No more tinsel on the carpet or fruitcake in the freezer. Our charge card was taking a much needed breather. We'd bought enough gifts to show our kids how much we love them (too much or not enough?). Our parental guilt was on hold for another year.

As native Nebraskans (you can take the Cornhusker out of the state but never the state out of the Cornhusker), Mark liked to take thirteen-year-old Carson to any of the Nebraska basketball games that came within free-throw distance of the Kansas City area where we lived. On this particular evening, the University of Nebraska was visiting the University of Kansas in nearby Lawrence.

As Mark and Carson headed for the game, Carson made good use of his holiday loot. His newest CD filled the car with a beat worthy of any pregame warm-up. He wore his Nebraska jacket and a pair of jeans that were new enough to still fit his sprouting frame. His athletic shoes were guaranteed to make him jump as high and run as fast as any NBA player. His red T-shirt was crisp (as T-shirts go) and as yet unfaded from a zillion washings. A baseball hat made hair combing as outdated as hair tonic.

The U.N.–K.U. game was the epitome of college basketball with the crowd properly loud, the cheerleaders properly agile, and the food properly empty of vitamins. "Go Big Red" ricocheted against "Rock Chalk Jayhawk." Fast-moving shoes squeaked against the varnished floor. The dribbled ball echoed. Claps and shouts.

Odd how a quiet moment can cut through the noise. Rise above it. A moment unplanned but forever remembered ...

After a proper refueling with Polish dogs and Coke at half-time, Carson pulled out his wallet.

Mark glanced over. "Isn't that my old wallet?" he asked.

Carson nodded. "You got a new one for Christmas. I took your old one. Is that OK?"

Mark shrugged and watched as Carson put his ticket stub in the wallet.

"What do you have in there?" Mark asked. "Lots of money?"

Carson spread the billfold. The only contents were ticket stubs from sporting events they had attended together.

"You've kept all those stubs? You've put them in my old wallet?"

"They're important to me," Carson said. "They help me remember. And I like having your old billfold better than any present I got for Christmas."

"Why?"

"Because it was yours."

Forget the team jackets, the CDs, the fancy athletic shoes ...

Our son is smart. Brilliant. A genius.

A blessing.

Amputating the Phone

Blessed is the man who perseveres under trial,
because when he has stood the test,
he will receive the crown of life that God has
promised to those who love him.

JAMES 1:12

I always wanted to be a surgeon—perform miracles, wear those cute little booties, cheat at golf. Trouble is, I get queasy cutting up a chicken, much less ...

But perhaps it's time for a career change. There is a definite need for some major surgery around our house—and it has nothing to do with my thighs. The catalyst for this switch is my youngest child and the telephone.

Laurel's a good girl. She gets A's in school and helps around the house with a tolerable amount of grumbling. She doesn't dress like Madonna and she occasionally chooses yogurt over potato chips. She prefers dropping her clothes on the floor rather than folding them—but who doesn't? Her main failing: she likes to talk on the phone—a lot.

I am not a phone person. When the phone rings I say what needs to be said and then I hang up. Laurel (and sister Emily before her) can find something to say to friends they were with ten minutes earlier. What do they discuss? The ride home? The weather at the friend's house versus ours? Although I show disdain for their actions in their presence, I am secretly amazed. If world leaders would talk to each other with as much passion and eye for detail as teens do, we'd have world peace by next Thursday.

At sixteen, Carson hasn't succumbed to the allure of the phone. But twelve-year-old Laurel makes up for it. I guess this proves the hypothesis that boys are slower in developing than girls. Thank goodness.

I've discovered some other strategies (short of amputating at the wrist) to free up the phone for the rest of us:

1. Make them talk within earshot. Parental presence is the best muzzle on the market. Long conversations suddenly become subdued with a lot of *um-hums* and *uh-uhs*. But smart kids eventually get around the restraints of listening ears. They work out a code. We finally caught on that Laurel's friend on the other end of the line was doing all the talking and asking all the pertinent questions while Laurel gave monosyllabic answers. After activating my code-breaking talents, I discovered that one grunt meant "I think he's cute" and two grunts meant "I haven't asked my parents if I can go to the pizza party Saturday night but I plan to as soon as I get off the phone." Become multilingual. It's very enlightening.

2. Set time limits. Never in my adult life have I encountered such a disparate view of the word "enough" as I did when we discussed telephone time limits. When Laurel and I first entered negotiations, I suggested fifteen minutes as a good time limit. My offering was met with a dropped jaw and a whining, "Mom!"

"Fine," I said. "What do you think is fair?"

Laurel counted on her fingers. "There's Courtney, Jess, and Rae Chelle ..."

"You see them at school."

"We can't talk about important stuff at school."

Ah, the *unimportant* halls of learning. "So how long do you need?"

Bad question. Too open-ended, giving Laurel hope that miracles do hap—

"Two hours should do it," she said.

Not bad. "Two hours a week should be agreeable," I said.

"Mom! I need two hours a *night!*"

My turn to gape. The negotiations dissolved faster than a snowball in Hades. We finally settled on one hour a night—all at once (for ease of regulation) and before 10:00 P.M. In my favor, I insisted on a stipulation that earned one last "Mom!" from Laurel: she couldn't talk on the phone at all until *after* her homework was done.

Rules are like pretzels: they're best when they're twisted. Laurel's logic: surely Mom can't object to me being on the phone if I'm using it to *do* homework? Studying together used to mean sitting next to each other at the kitchen table. Now, the kids sit at the kitchen table or the computer—in two different houses—connected by the phone glued to their ears. All the better to hear you with, my dear.

3. Get call waiting. When Laurel is on the phone and someone tries to call in, she hears a muffled beep on the line. By pushing the hang-up button she can put her current call on hold and answer the second one. The rule is, if a call comes in for someone else in the family, Laurel has to hang up on her friend and let us take it. Actually, she's pretty good about this. But there is one odd aspect of this technical miracle—we never hear the phone ring anymore. "Mom, get the phone!" is hollered from an upper floor with no forewarning. It's spooky.

4. Get a second phone line. A last resort and one I'm not willing to visit. It's not a question of the extra money (well, maybe it is). It's a matter of control. Somehow, giving a child a personal phone line is tantamount to surrender. Might as well give me a pair of earmuffs and a blindfold so I'm deaf, blind, and dumb. Might as well give the kid her own home with her own phone line and her own bills to pay and ...

Before I snap up that last intriguing option I remind myself that Laurel will be on her own soon enough. There might come a time when I'll actually miss her telephone exploits.

Until then, a surgeon's work is never done.

It's My Job

I prayed for this child, and the Lord has granted me what I asked of him. So now I give him to the Lord.

1 SAMUEL 1:27-28

Emily was supposed to be on a plane to Germany. So why was she calling me from Beloit, Wisconsin?

"You're where?" I asked.

"The flight was canceled till tomorrow. A bird flew into the engine." She conveyed this information with as much ease as if the bird were an invited guest. "They bused us from Chicago to a motel in Beloit. We're staying overnight."

The bombshell came next.

"There was an odd number of girls in our group so I get a room all to myself."

My stomach did the tango. My little girl (who had somehow turned sixteen while my back was turned) was being forced to stay alone in a motel room in a strange town, in a strange state (I apologize to Beloit and Wisconsin).

"Are you scared?" I asked, assuming she wanted some motherly reassurance.

"Of course not," she said. "It's cool. We have to leave for the new flight at three in the morning so we're going to stay up all night and go swimming and—"

"At least you have your luggage."

"No … just my carry-on."

"Then how are you going to go swimming?" My mind conjured up a compound word that started with *skinny-* and ended with *-dip.*

"We're going to swim in our clothes."

I put my Reassurance button on hold and engaged my Oh-No-You-Don't switch. I reminded Emily she would be traveling thirteen hours in those clothes and would be wearing those same clothes when she met the host family she would be staying with for her three-week stay in Germany. I pointed out that a chlorine-encrusted T-shirt was apt to take on a life of its own.

Her response to my Oh-No-You-Don't wisdom?

"Oh, yeah. Maybe I won't."

Good choice.

After letting my fears volley back and forth with her sense of adventure in a quick match of mother-daughter banter, Emily told me to quit worrying.

"I can't," I said. "It's my job."

We said our goodbyes and hung up. I started to cry.

Up to this point I had accepted the opportunity of Emily's trip to Germany with an amazing amount of restraint. Emily had soothed my phobias with nary a whimper. She let me pack the extra socks (you can't have too many socks or underwear); the telephone numbers of Aunts Crystie and Lois, Uncle Tom, and the neighbor who says hello when I take my walk (just in case); an assortment of cookies, crackers, and candies (since everyone knows there is no food in Germany); and a picture of her family in case she had the gall to forget our beaming faces. Germany was an accepted fact. Germany, I could handle.

Being laid over in Beloit was beyond my comprehension.

She was out of my reach. She was out of my control. She was truly on her own.

I confined myself to a two-tissue cry. Then I did what I should have done in the first place. I prayed.

"Lord, Emily's alone and scared." I quickly made an amendment. "Actually Emily's alone and I'm the one who's scared. Since I can't be with her, I give her to you. Please, take care of her."

Two days later we heard from Emily. She was safe in Germany, in another family's care. The group had a great time in Beloit, watching movies, eating pizza, and getting to know each other. And no, they did not go swimming in their clothes—or otherwise.

I relaxed. For the moment. Only nineteen more days and she'd be mine again.

In the meantime, God would take care of her for me.

After all, it's his job.

The Golden Silence

Sons are a heritage from the Lord,
children a reward from him.

PSALM 127:3

Iunderstand children are a gift from God—but that doesn't stop me from suffering moments when I'd like a refund. Or an exchange. Maybe one child for two cats and a gerbil. Or a rabbit. Rabbits would be good. They're quiet. They don't eat much and they let you hold them on your lap without squirming away.

And they don't walk like elephants. Only elephants—and my children—walk like elephants. There is a law of physics that applies here: the smaller the child, the louder the footsteps. A sixty-pound nine-year-old running through the living room has the ability to make our best china rattle like a 7.1 earthquake—aftershocks inevitable. Inversely, a 120-pound teen of sixteen can move from front door to bedroom so silently I'll raise my head like a doe in the forest, sure something has just passed close but unsure of its intent.

My children are destined for the theater. "PLEASE PASS THE POTATOES" is delivered loudly enough to be heard in the back row of any auditorium. The discussion that follows regarding whose turn it is to clear the dishes is worthy of a Laurel and Hardy skit (and we even have our own Laurel).

I love my three kids dearly. Yet sometimes I yearn for "a time to be silent."

One weekend, I got my wish—though I had to get sick to do it.

75

We were scheduled to drive to our hometown of Lincoln, Nebraska, to go to a Cornhusker football game. But when I woke up Saturday morning, the glands in my neck made me resemble a chipmunk stocking up for the winter. Not wanting to ruin everyone's fun, I sent my family north, checked with a doctor, got a prescription, and settled into our empty house.

Our silent empty house.

No elephant footfalls. No "But Mom, he did it first!" No slammed doors, Scooby Doo, or the wails of Carson practicing his trumpet (exactly who or what is wailing is an important differentiation).

The ticking of the clock in the entry. The hmmm of the refrigerator. The whoosh of the furnace making me feel cozy warm as I snuggled beneath an afghan on the couch.

"This is the life," I told the air. "I can do what I want, when I want to do it. I can eat foods that have no nutritional value. I can watch old movies on TV with no one moaning about the lack of special effects. I can read. I can take a nap. I can take a bath with no interruptions."

And self-serving hedonist that I am, I did all of those things, reveling in the solitude with as much ecstasy as Scrooge McDuck swimming in his vault of gold coins.

But after my dinner of chocolate chocolate-chip ice cream and Diet Coke; after watching *An Affair to Remember* and *Rear Window*; after crying over Father Ralph de Bricassart's death in *The Thorn Birds*; and after a bath where I emerged a prune, I took another listen to the silence I'd wrapped around myself. I found it wanting.

I missed the rumble as Emily hurtled down the stairs in her combat boots. I missed Carson's humming as he made a batch of chocolate-drop cookies, along with a mess in the kitchen. I missed the sound of Laurel reading aloud to her invisible class as she played school. And our king-sized bed seemed empty without its king.

With the noises of night closing in around me, I imagined a life without the sounds of my children. The sounds of their gentle snores when they were safely tucked in bed. Their three voices merged as they said grace before a meal. I imagined never hearing the title "Mom," whether it was tagged on a request for a ride to school or on the thank-you after giving the ride.

As I tried to get to sleep I found the silence heavy—the silence that *could have been* if we *hadn't been* blessed with three children. I turned on the television for company and fell asleep to the canned sounds of voices, footfalls, and the rattling of TV people going through the process of living.

When my family returned the next day, bursting in with thudding feet, overlapping voices, and gusts of fall air, I was ready for them. Renewed. Patient again—at least for a little while.

In the stillness of my weekend I found that silence is indeed golden. For it reminded me of something very important.

My children are more precious than gold.

Call on Me

For when I am weak, then I am strong.

2 CORINTHIANS 12:10

It was not a phone call I wanted to get. My son's teacher was calling: Carson was missing six assignments. He had two A's and six zeros, which averaged out to ... trouble.

I summoned my husband, Mark. I interrupted Carson's game of Frisbee. Mark and I pointed to the couch. Carson slunk into the cushions like a puppy who'd chewed his master's shoe. We sat across from him, our arms crossed in our best judge and jury stance.

"What's going on, Carson?"

Consider the fact he was thirteen. What was his answer?

a.) "I don't know."
b.) "I don't know." Or
c.) "I don't know."

If you guessed correctly, you are either a parent or you remember being thirteen yourself.

Actually, after we got past the I-don't-know answer, we discovered the reason he had neglected to turn in those six assignments—and believe it or not, it had nothing to do with a dog eating his homework. His closet ate it (but that's another story).

To summarize, Carson needed to get organized.

I embarrass my son by writing this to avoid embarrassing myself. His weakness of not being organized is no worse than

78

my weakness of impatience, or my husband's weakness of pro-crastination, or my daughter's weakness of … my, my, we are a flawed bunch, aren't we?

That's my point.

For the rest of the evening, Carson was the quintessential martyr. He moped around the house brandishing his calling card, "Hi, my name is Carson and I have to get my life together." The thought was good but the martyr routine got old faster than a "Brady Bunch" rerun. He seemed to enjoy making his failing a national concern.

Another chat was in order. A let's-get-this-in-perspective chat. For this installment of my questionable parental wisdom, I chose the great outdoors. Somehow, talking about God and prayer seemed more appropriate in the presence of stars and a crescent moon rather than yesterday's newspaper and a laundry basket full of fifty-seven unmatched socks.

"There's something you need to do, Carson," I said, sitting down on the front step.

He interrupted with his slogan, "I have to get my life—"

"Your life is fine," I said. "At the moment you have a problem."

"Two problems—you forgot my closet."

I could *never* forget his closet.

I stilled his hands, which were dissecting a sprig of yew. "How do you think Dad feels when you come to him and say, 'Hey, Dad, can you show me how to pitch the baseball really fast? Please, Dad. Can you help me?'"

"He feels good."

"Because you need him."

"I do."

I waved my arm to take in the sky. "God's the Father of all fathers, the best there is. And he loves to hear his children say, 'Please, God. Can you help me?'"

"It makes him feel good?"

"Because you need him."

I touched his legs—the legs that would soon be as long as mine. "Give your problem to God. Tell him you can't handle it alone and you need his help."

Carson smiled. "Will he do my homework for me?"

I tousled his hair.

The next day Carson finished his school work—and cleaned out his closet. I'd love to report he was the epitome of organization from that point on, but I can't. Just as I can't report that I didn't lose my patience today when the garage door refused to work—the garage door Mark's been meaning to fix....

But we'll make it—weaknesses and all.

God's ready to help. All we have to do is ask.

Asking or Telling?

I know that even now God will give you whatever you ask.

JOHN 11:22

Seventeen-year-old Emily grabbed her school books, her jacket, and my sanity, and headed for the door.

"Bye, I'm going," she said, brushing past me in a gust of teenage energy.

"Bye," I said. "Have a good day at—"

She stopped. Backtracked two steps. Faced me. "By the way," she said. "I'm going to Homecoming Saturday. Sarah and I are going to buy a dress after school." She took a step toward the door before adding, "On Saturday, we'll be out really late because after the dance we're going to some haunted houses."

"In your fancy clothes?"

"Of course not," Emily said. "We're going to change into jeans."

Silly me. I should have realized a Homecoming dance and Halloween suspense were natural companions. I pushed the illogic of her plans aside. There was something else that bothered me more than the mixture of glitz and ghouls.

"Are you asking me or telling me?"

Gotcha. Her left eyebrow raised an inch, then lowered as she regrouped. "I'm asking. I just wanted you to know the details."

"Um-hm."

"Really," she said, taking a backward step toward the door and freedom.

"Um-hm," I said again, enjoying the renewed feeling of control (however false).

She shifted her books to the other arm. "Well? Can I go? Please?"

I pretended to consider, making her squirm a bit as a penalty for her indiscretion. "I suppose," I said. "But you'll be home by midnight. No later."

She cocked her head, then straightened it as she realized a partial victory was better than none. She pivoted and headed toward the door, the spring in her step marking her success.

"But, Emily?" I said, stopping her retreat. "Next time, ask. Really ask."

She gave me a knowing smile and left.

I poured another cup of coffee and headed to my computer, my thoughts moving from Emily's methods—to my own. I had been working on an assigned article and it wasn't going well. I'd already rewritten it three times, from three different approaches, and I was weary of it. Truth be told, I wanted it to go away. Yet none of the drafts seemed right. I *wanted* them to be right. I *willed* them to be right, but ...

I settled in and took a sip of caffeine, hoping it would jump-start some glimmer of inspiration. I opened the file on the first draft. Maybe it would read better today. Maybe somehow, something miraculous had happened within the workings of the computer overnight and it was suddenly good.

Without even realizing what I was doing, I said a prayer. "Can one of these drafts be acceptable?" I said aloud. "Can one of them be good enough? I want to move on to something—"

I stopped in mid-sentence, my mouth hanging open. *Was I asking or telling? Was I asking God for permission to do what I'd already made up my mind to do? Was I wanting a blessing on MY will instead of asking for the implementation of HIS will?* Was I treating my Heavenly Father exactly as Emily had treated her very earthly mother?

Oops.

I took a cleansing breath and read through the drafts. One, two, three strikes, you're out. I opened a new file, the whiteness of the screen challenging me, daring me to see beyond my own plans of quick and easy and to face the fact that my way was not the best way. I closed my eyes. This time the prayer was simpler, less specific, giving space for God's will instead of my own.

"Help me," I said. Asked.

And like the loving Father he is, God answered.

They're Touching Me!

Therefore encourage each other.

1 THESSALONIANS 4:18

Vacations are a time of relaxation and togetherness. A time to get to know your family, to talk, to laugh, to ... hold back a primal scream.

I shouldn't complain. Not everyone has to—I mean, gets to—travel during their time off from work. Some people get to—I mean, have to—stay home and watch "Columbo" reruns while they clean out a few drawers.

Being together is good ... although our annual eleven-hour drive to the mountains of Colorado does tend to test the concept.

On this particular trip, it only took minutes before Mark and I exchanged a frenzied look that asked, *Why did we trade in the minivan?* It must have been temporary insanity—or vanity. The minivan, although lacking the misbegotten elegance of the car we now drove, had one very important vacation necessity: space. One peek into the backseat revealed three kids plastered shoulder to shoulder (or was that Carson's knee against Emily's shoulder?). They were so close I could reach back and touch them—a scary thought considering they could reciprocate. And the treasures that were transferred over the seat? Their garbage was our garbage: sticky candy wrappers, broken crayons, used Kleenex.

Even the sacred Goody Bag lost some of its appeal when the goodies were doled out in such cramped quarters.

Being close enough to touch another human being who is a member of one's own family is the true test of a vacation. As the mile markers whizzed by, the back seat battle cry began, its merciless repetition bouncing off the windshield and my peace of mind.

"Mom! They're touching me!"

Before flipping a coin to see which child got the back seat alone while we relegated one sibling to the trunk and another to the top carrier (or before *I* volunteered), I took evasive action. As our family rule is he-who-drives-calls-the-shots, I offered to take the wheel. I immediately christened it nap time. "Dad needs to sleep," I said. *And I need ten miles of silence.* It took five miles of grumbling for the kids to get comfortable. I basked in the peace. Even the guttural snores of my husband were music. Six miles. Seven ... Laurel sneezed. Her elbow bumped into Carson's ear. Carson's knee rammed into Emily's cheek.

"Oww!"

"Stop that!"

"Mom! They're touching—"

Daytime talk shows looked like prayer meetings compared to the interpersonal relationships tested in our car.

Music soothes the savage ... I put in a cassette.

So began the battle of the bands. Garth Brooks versus Wayne Watson. Metallica took on Mariah Carey and Les Misérables. And the winner was ...

Fifteen minutes of each. We developed a keen awareness of how interminable fifteen minutes feels when it's spent listening to someone else's favorite music (especially when that someone sings along).

Eons later we staggered into my parents' Colorado cabin and collapsed into the blessed sleep of the car-less.

The first day dawned, greeting us with something foreign. Silence. No computer, cable TV, stereo, answering machine, or Nintendo violated the mountain air.

Just us. Twenty-four hours a day. Dawn to yawn. The personal boundaries that were tested in the car were expanded within the confines of the cabin—but were soon sorely pressed. Five people sharing one bathroom. Five snores bouncing off the open rafters in a nocturnal duel. The patter of rain on the roof making the walls inch closer.

"We can't even go outside," Laurel said. She stood at the kitchen window watching a chipmunk run for cover.

I handed her a dish towel, making her regret her close proximity to chores.

"We can do what I used to do with my mother," I said. "She would wash the dishes and one of us kids would dry. Then she would—"

"You didn't have a dishwasher?"

I held up my sudsy hands. "Just these."

"You must have been poor."

Not at all.

I thought back to my mother testing our spelling abilities as we shared the chores after dinner. I'd learned to spell "Kennedy" with a dish towel in my hands.

"Spell 'mountain,'" I said.

"That's easy," Laurel said, "M-o-u-n-t-a-i-n."

"How about 'continental divide'?"

She looked to the ceiling for help. "C-o-n ..."

Emily and Carson came in to see what we were doing. The

difficulty of the spelling words increased to match their added competition.

As we finished the dishes and declared a three-way tie, we lingered a little, unwilling to relinquish this unexpected bit of togetherness. The cry of "they're touching me" was noticeably absent.

Odd how it took the constraints of a small cabin six hundred miles from home for us to realize another facet of that much-maligned phrase.

It's true, it's all true. They're touching me.

The Crack of a Bat

You will understand what is right and just and fair— every good path.

PROVERBS 2:9

The bleachers are packed, shoulder to shoulder. My pop has lost its fizz. There's a mustard stain on my shorts from the hot dog I've devoured in six bites. The wind is holding its breath—along with the crowd.

The crack of a bat. We stand in unison, our eyes straining to see the white ball against the blue sky.

It's caught. Bobbled. Dropped.

"Run!"

First base is history. The runner rounds second heading for third. The ball slices through the air beside him, racing him to the bag. The third baseman stands ready, one foot on the base, mitt set. Suddenly, the mitt is raised higher. Higher. The baseman jumps for the ball as it's thrown over his head.

"Go!"

The bleachers clang and clatter as I wave my arms and run the last stretch with him as he safely crosses home plate!

My son.

And to think I knew him a lifetime ago when he wore tennies with He-Man printed on the sides. Or not so long ago, when he stumbled over air if nothing else was in his way.

Our family's been through it all: tee-ball, softball, baseball. I will never forget Carson at age six, scurrying around the field, learning to play the game. His T-shirt hung over his ever-scraped knees, his shoelaces were untied, and we were just as apt to see him sitting on the field poking a friendly bug as running the bases.

Running the bases was confusing to Carson. He knew it had something to do with hitting the ball with that bat-thingy, but if by some miracle this actually happened, he would freeze. His eyes would get as big as the ball and his mouth would gape like a codfish.

Now what do I do? He would look to the crowd for guidance.

I'd spring out of my lawn chair, pump my hand in the air, and shriek, "Go! Go!" Carson would raise his shoulders to ask, "Where? Where?" Mark (who was also the coach) pointed the way toward first base. Carson ran in that approximate direction—probably because it was *away* from my frenzy.

During all of this commotion—which took approximately two days—you'd think there would have been ample time for the ball to be fielded and thrown to first base. Theoretically, it should have been waiting for Carson when Mark pushed him the final few feet toward the bag.

Wrong.

The ball was still sitting where it had rolled—two feet in front of home plate. The infield players had made no move to retrieve it. They were too busy scanning the crowd, trying to decipher what *their* parents' shouts of "Go! Go!" were supposed to mean.

It was exhausting. At least for us parents. Especially since we were the only ones who cared who won. Carson was more concerned with getting his very own can of Dr. Pepper at the end of the game—or better yet, a Nerds Blizzard at Dairy Queen.

As Carson got older, he graduated to learning the finer points of the game. Namely that it's easier to catch the ball if you don't close your eyes, and that cute girls, standing on the other side of the fence (even ones with their teeth in braces), can be just as distracting as a friendly bug.

I did my own graduating—from sitting on a lawn chair in a grassy field to sitting on bleachers at a field complex with lights, a bullpen, and hot dogs. Games were extended from one hour where Carson would whine, "I'm tired, can we go home now?" to two hours where I would whine, "I'm tired, can we go home now?"

Carson's games might not have had the organ music or dancing fountains of the pros (and certainly not the strikes and the salaries), but baseball *has* taught him these important life lessons:

Number One, it's not polite to pick your nose in public.

Number Two, everyone gets a turn (even Tommy-who-lives-down-the-street who couldn't hit the ball if it were glued to the bat).

And finally, the all-important Number Three—win or lose, when everything's over, you have to show enough character to file past your opponents, look them in the eye, and say "good game."

Not bad.

Get me another hot dog. And don't you dare hold the mustard.

Drinking It In

May your father and your mother be glad;
may she who gave you birth rejoice!

PROVERBS 23:25

The clock struck two. The kids were in school. The house was quiet except for the rain pattering against the windows. I shared the last of my tuna sandwich with the cats sitting at my feet. It was time to tackle the next item on my to-do list. This afternoon I was going to organize six months' worth of photos into albums. I carried the packets to the table. I got out the new albums—and a few old ones.

Memory lane invited me to take a stroll.

There was Emily on the first day of kindergarten, her skin tanned and her hair bleached from summer playing. Carson wearing a beanie with a whirling propeller, holding his blankie. Laurel showing off a new pair of shoes, the white rubber toes gleaming along with her smile.

So small. So long ago. And yet, only yesterday.

When had they grown up?

The photos took me captive. These weren't my kids. Surely, my children were never so young. So innocent. So needing. But there *I* was in a photo, helping Laurel blow out some birthday candles. I was there. I had lived it too. *Why was it so hard to remember?*

"I was busy," I said out loud.

The words echoed off the stack of dishes on the counter and came back to my ears sounding false. Of course I was busy.

With one child I was busy. With two I was busy. With three I was busy. With all of them off at school I was still busy. It was a poor excuse.

I flipped the pages. Carson's first bike. Laurel's first doll. Emily's first dance. So many firsts had been captured on film. Three lifetimes of firsts. Yet I couldn't remember reveling in these milestones. They came, were noted, and life went on. Was I too busy thinking of the age they'd *be* to appreciate the age they *were*?

I remembered saying to Emily: "You can drive a car when you're sixteen."

To Carson: "You can mow the lawn when you're twelve."

To Laurel: "You can go to the neighborhood pool without me when you're nine."

Thinking of future events. Future times. But what about *now*?

Thinking of the future wasn't all bad. Having goals. Making plans. Striving for the next milestone. But what had I missed— what had we all missed—in not savoring the present with as much fervor as we relished the future?

I paused at a photo of my mother reading Emily a book. Emily's tiny finger pointed at a picture on the first page. *One fish, two fish, red fish, blue fish.* Calm. Close. Caring.

Maybe that was the advantage of being a grandparent. They could take the time to see—really see—the children. They watched. They noticed. They drank it in.

They didn't have to worry about scheduling a dentist appointment for Emily, getting a pair of black pants for Carson before the band concert (since he'd already sprouted out of the other "new" pair); picking up a red three-ring notebook for Laurel's science—

Picking up!

I looked out the window at the rain. The clock started its chime. I had to pick Carson up from school or he'd start walking and be soaked by the time he got home. I grabbed my keys and searched for some shoes. Any shoes ... if only Carson were old enough to drive—

I stopped with one shoe on.

Don't think that way. Appreciate him at fourteen. He will never be fourteen again. When he's fifteen he might not pop in the door after school and yell, "Hi-dee-ho, Mama-jo." He might not give me an awkward hug before he goes to bed at night. He might not ...

I pulled next to Carson as he started walking home in the rain.

"Hi-dee-ho, Mama-jo," he said as he got in the car. "Thanks for the ride."

"It's my pleasure," I said. And I meant it.

Needful Things

Let the sea resound, and everything in it,
the world, and all who live in it.
Let the rivers clap their hands,
let the mountains sing together for joy;
let them sing before the Lord,
for he comes to judge the earth.
He will judge the world in righteousness
and the peoples with equity.

PSALM 98:7-9

I may complain about my kids' attitudes, and poke fun at their teen stereotypes (after all, stereotypes are stereotypes because they tend to be true). Yet to extend that truth I've got to admit that I've worn a bit of teenage attitude in my time—although it was garbed in polyester instead of cotton. Case in point: one teenager and one mountain in Colorado....

Long's Peak is the highest peak in Rocky Mountain National Park. But it was only slightly higher than the ego of an eighteen-year-old. The ego belonged to me.

As a senior in high school, I *knew* the world was small—it extended only as far as my eyes and arms could reach. The world revolved around me. The fact that Long's Peak rose 14,255 feet above sea level was merely a statistic to add to my bank of knowledge. Climbing it would be no big deal.

A very big deal.

For eleven months out of the year, I lived with my parents in Lincoln, Nebraska, fourteen thousand feet below the summit of

Long's Peak. For one month every summer we left the plains behind and drove the five hundred miles to our cabin in Colorado. Sweltering heat and humidity were exchanged for cool nights and pine-scented breezes. It took a few days for our lungs to adjust to the thinner air and a few more days for our legs to adjust to walking on land that wasn't flat.

Hiking was a requisite. Two or three times a week we got up at dawn (so we'd be back before the midday rain shower), drove to a trail head, and hiked three or four miles to a pristine mountain lake. I liked walking through the forests, surrounded by the wilderness that had let me in to visit. I felt a kinship with nature as I sat on a boulder beside a lake. The walls of the mountains were mighty guards against the outside world. I was at home. I felt welcome.

But each year Long's Peak—and its fourteen-mile trek—teased us. There were few places around our cabin where its looming presence didn't taunt us. Its perfection was like a picture postcard, the afternoon clouds breaking against its peaks, adjusting themselves for the next photographer's dream.

When some Colorado friends said they were going to climb it and invited me along, the gauntlet was thrown. There was no way I wouldn't go. Mom and Dad decided to take the challenge with me. If they wanted to come, fine. But I could handle it alone. *I didn't need them.*

We took a few days to plan our journey, which would include an overnight camp at a halfway point called Jim's Grove. We read books that spoke of strange-sounding landmarks: the Boulder Field, the Trough, the Homestretch. Mention of people who'd had trouble climbing Long's Peak—people losing their lives or breaking various limbs—made me respect, but not fear, this wonder of nature. I was quick to note that most of these victims had been attempting technical climbs, not sticking to the trail like we would be doing.

The trouble was, after getting halfway up the mountain, there *wasn't* a trail.

We were used to the nicely sculpted dirt paths maintained by the park service. A few stones and exposed tree roots would force us to watch our footing, but they were not enough to distract us from the aromatic shelter of pine trees and the chattering company of chipmunks darting among the wildflowers.

But as we cleared timberline at eleven thousand feet, there was no dirt path. No path of any kind. There were no trees. The air was so thin the only plant life that could survive was low-growing plants and lichen clinging to the rocks. And the rocks went on forever. The "trail" was marked by cairns—man-made mounds of stones—balancing on top of the boulders.

We had reached the Boulder Field. Acres and acres of man-sized boulders stretched between us and the peak, boulders tossed a millennium ago as God shaped the mountain to his liking.

Although I tried to keep up with my friends, their mountain legs were stronger than my flatland legs and I fell behind. Reluctantly, I walked with my parents, our eyes forced downward as we negotiated boulder after boulder. Our breath could not be wasted with talk as our lungs worked overtime, gasping for oxygen in the thin air.

"Stop," my mother said, after scrambling over the boulders for a half hour. She sank onto a rock to catch her breath. Dad and I joined her.

I took a swig of water from my canteen. Then I looked around in a panic. "There are no more streams," I said. "Where are we going to get water?"

My father scanned the boulders. "Snow," he said, pointing toward the peak.

Huge glaciers hugged the sides of the mountain up ahead. Under the August sun their melting trickle joined with other trickles to form the rushing streams that sped down the mountains. Streams into rivers. Rivers into oceans.

Eating snow? I thought. I can do without it. *I don't need—*

My friends were small dots against the boulders far ahead. I held up a finger, blotting them out. Yet the immensity of the mountain couldn't be blotted out with a finger. Not with an entire hand. I looked back to where we had been—and ahead to where we had to go. My teenage bravado left me. I was insignificant. A mere dot on the face of God's earth.

"My legs hurt," I said, looking for an excuse. "And I'm tired. And hungry. And—"

"You're not giving up, are you?" asked Mom.

I shrugged. "It's too much," I said.

Dad stood and pulled me to standing. "No," he said. "It's just enough."

He wouldn't let me turn back. We trudged forward. *Maybe I did need them.*

More than an hour later we gazed upon our next obstacle. The Trough. The Boulder Field was nothing compared to this. At a seam where one mountain peak met another, an avalanche of boulders had been strewn like so many misshapen monster-sized marbles. The cairns were gone. Now painted bull's-eyes marked our way. Up.

"We're supposed to go up there?" I asked, pointing to the top of the Trough, hundreds of feet straight up the tower of tumbled stones.

I saw the first hint of doubt in my mother's eyes. Dad leaned his hands on his knees, panting for air. I recognized their look of surrender. I'd felt it before. Now they ...

They needed me. I pointed to the top. "We can do it. It can't be much farther," I said. "We're running out of mountain."

Dad straightened. "I'm beginning to think we'll never run out of mountain."

"I'll go first," I said. And they followed.

Instead of merely hiking across the face of boulders as we had done on the Boulder Field, we were forced to scramble up the rocks of the Trough using our hands. Our knees. Our toes.

I kept looking back, checking on my parents. I wasn't particularly worried about Dad, but Mom had never had the greatest balance. One rock at a time, Dad climbed ahead and held his hand for Mom to take. Guiding her. Helping her. *They needed each other.*

I had no concept of time. All my concentration went toward the next step. The next foothold. The next moment of rest when I could stand straight, arch my back, and grab a mouthful of air.

We reached the top of the Trough. My friends were waiting for me.

"Come on," they said. "It's just along this ledge and then up Homestretch to the summit."

I saw Mom studying the ledge we had to traverse. Two feet wide with a sheer mountain face rising to the left—and falling into oblivion to the right. Falling ... not a good word.

"I'm not going any farther," she said.

"But, Mom—"

She sat down on a rock. "I'm not." Her voice wasn't full of frustration or fatigue as mine had been when I'd threatened to give up on the Boulder Field. Her voice was full of instinct and conviction. "This is as far as I'm supposed to go."

Dad took a seat beside her. "She's right," he said. "We'll wait here. You go ahead."

My friends had already started on the ledge, their steps small by necessity. Their left hands caressed the face of the mountain, giving them a false sense of safety. I looked to them. I looked to my parents.

"I'll stay too," I said.

Mom took a deep breath and gazed across the layers of mountains extending below us. We could see the flat stretch of the prairie miles and miles away. The Boulder Field looked like a mere scattering of pebbles.

"We climbed all this way together," she said. "You need to go the rest of the way on your own."

I needed to stay with my parents. Where it was safe.

"Come on, Nancy," called my friends.

"Go," said my dad.

I needed to—

"You'll wait for me?" I asked.

"Of course we will," said Mom. "We'll be right here for you."

And they were. Just as they'd always been.

I climbed to the top of Long's Peak. I wrote my name in the book that held testament to all who'd come before me. I looked over the world, touching the sky, being as high as I could be without God pulling me higher.

A conqueror.

But I wasn't a conqueror. For I had not reached the mountaintop on my own. I had needed my parents, just as they had needed me. When the time came, they had urged me to go farther still. They had released me into the custody of my friends. And now as our goal had been achieved, as we spread out across the rocky peak, my friends released me to God, to witness his awesome spectacle seen from the top of a mountain.

My world was larger now. For in the perfection that was laid out before me, I caught a glimpse of a masterpiece. Not a masterpiece created by mankind—especially not a cocky eighteen-year-old. But a masterpiece created by the Master himself.

I was not the center of this world. God was. God stood beside me on *his* mountaintop. *His* sun warmed my face and *his* winds tangled my hair.

And then I knew. I could not do it alone. I needed them all. My family. My friends. And my God.

May my children learn the same lesson, on their own mountain.

Now and Then

There is a time for everything,
and a season for every activity under heaven.
ECCLESIASTES 3:1

Carson came downstairs carrying a buffalo, a walrus, and three dinosaurs.

"What are you doing?" I asked, petting the stuffed buffalo which had sat on his dresser for years.

"I'm cleaning," he said.

Without being told? I kept my sarcasm to myself. "So why are you bringing your animals down here?"

"I'm grown up now," he said. "I don't notice them anymore. They're just *there*, taking up space." He picked a piece of dust off the buffalo's nose. "I really like these guys, but now..." He touched the tail of the tyrannosaurus rex.

Maybe it *was* time for a change. I opened the doors of the buffet and began pulling out long-forgotten knickknacks. Here was a red, yellow, and blue trivet that had matched our first kitchen. It had hung on a cup hook above the stove. I scraped my fingernail against some long-dried spaghetti sauce. The trivet certainly had no place in my current navy and salmon decor.

And look, there was a teacup painted with purple violets. It had been displayed on our dresser back when the kids were small. Now, purple was not welcome in our home. Neither was the wooden "M" painted with daisies, or the rather shabby cream and sugar I'd bought for $1.25 at a garage sale.

I set the forgotten treasures on the buffet and stepped back. They were worthless; they held no monetary value. I'd be lucky to get $1.25 for the lot. Yet, each in its own time had held a place of honor in our home. We had looked at them with appreciation and satisfaction. They had been important to us once.

But then we had replaced them with other treasures ... just like Carson was replacing his stuffed animals with ... whatever would next appear on his dresser.

Carson came back into the room, his arms empty.

"Where did you put your animals?" I asked.

"In my box in the basement."

"You're not giving them away?"

He shrugged. "I don't think so. Just because I don't want them out doesn't mean I don't care about them. They bring back memories."

He left me with *my* memories—which I promptly returned to their hideaway in the buffet.

Just because they didn't fit into our lives anymore didn't mean they weren't a part of us. The trivet, the teacup, the "M," and the cream and sugar would always hold a place in my heart, if not on my mantel.

When I was finished, I looked at my present pretties with new appreciation: the rose plate, the candleholder, and the ostrich fan. Their worth was not measured in their cost, nor in their impact on our lives. They were merely "things." And yet their existence marked a moment. Like the lost treasures of an ancient pyramid, these possessions were proof that a family had lived here—was growing older here. They were proof we had been blessed in many, many ways.

I had much to be thankful for, if only I took the time to open my eyes and notice.

The Reading Contest

Train a child in the way he should go,
and even when he is old he will not turn from it.

PROVERBS 22:6

A strange circular glow shone through Laurel's blanket.

"What are you doing?" I asked. "It's after eleven."

Her head popped out from the covers. The glow mysteriously disappeared. I held out my hand. Reluctantly, she relinquished her flashlight.

"But, Mom," she whined. "I just had to see if Lucy gets back through the wardrobe."

I held out my other hand and waited for Laurel to give up C.S. Lewis' *The Lion, the Witch and the Wardrobe.*

I slipped the book under my arm and tucked her in. "Lucy will be fine," I said. "I guarantee it."

Getting Laurel to read was not a problem. My other two children were another story. They supported the rule that no two children in any one family can be alike. At fifteen, Emily complained she was too busy with friends, her part-time job, and school (did I mention friends?) to read for fun. Carson, who at twelve thought any activity that didn't involve a ball was boring, regarded having to read as a punishment worse than fouling out of a basketball game.

How to get my three dissimilar children to read books became a quest deserving a government grant.

The solution was: a Contest.

"Whoever reads the most books in the next three months

will win a reading contest," I announced while loading the dishwasher one evening.

Emily's face clouded. "That's not fair," she said. "Laurel's books are shorter than mine."

She was right.

We pondered this dilemma a moment. It was Carson, in a spurt of sportsmanlike conduct, who came up with the answer.

"Whoever reads the most *pages* wins," he suggested.

Perfect.

They wrote their names atop three sheets of paper and attached them to the back of the laundry room door. There, they would list their books and the page length.

"What do we win?" asked Laurel.

The ideal prize revealed itself in a moment of parental brilliance.

"The first place winner gets $10.00 to spend at a bookstore. Second place gets $7.50 and third place gets $5.00."

We had a winner.

The kids are now heavily into the fourth year of their contests (which usually last three or four months each) and can confirm they are a blazing success. Each child—even Carson, the sports fiend—has won the contest at least once. Their bookshelves display their winnings like trophies.

But the best part?

All of us are winners.

Time Travel

The child grew and was weaned, and on the day
Isaac was weaned Abraham held a great feast.

GENESIS 21:8

Our kids don't need me anymore. They know how to tie their shoes, comb their hair, and they can easily reach the top shelf of the coat closet without my assistance. They know the state capitals, how to wash their whites and colored clothes separately and how to download, upload and sideload the computer.

It's said that as our Father, God wants us to need him—depend on him. I understand this need. Sometimes I miss my kids' dependence. The good old days, when the first word uttered every morning was, "Mommy!" I controlled every morsel of food that went into their mouths. I chose their clothes and made sure their socks matched. When I was cold, they wore a jacket. When I was tired, they took a nap. I determined what TV shows were appropriate, which friends were well enough behaved, and how to spend the birthday money they got from Grandma Swenson.

Although I might have complained about the responsibility, deep down, I relished the control. These little people needed me. They looked up to me. They respected and loved me. I was head honcho, overseer, and queen of the little bees. I was Mom.

Then they grew up. It came as a shock. It's not that I didn't notice it along the way but … I didn't. One day they were making motor-sounds as they pushed a car under my feet while I made dinner and the next they were making motor-sounds as they drove their car *out* to dinner (and I wasn't invited).

I went from being one of the most important people in their lives to being one of the least—

No. I won't say that. It's not true. It can't be true. Just because my kids are growing into independent people who can handle the day-to-day doings of their lives without my assistance doesn't mean I'm not important to them anymore.

Does it?

But what can I give them now? I used to be able to show my love by being essential in their lives. They needed me. I needed them. Now that they are away from the house nearly as much as they are home, how can I show my love? What's the common denominator between then and now?

Time. Although much has changed in the nineteen years since we had Emily (sixteen for Carson and twelve for Laurel), God still provides twenty-four hours in a day. And though the kids aren't beside me as much (why did I used to call it "under-foot"?), there are still plenty of minutes to spend together. Perhaps the minutes can be even better spent, as we don't have to deal with the logistics of naps and baths (all right, it still comes up occasionally). We can concentrate on getting to know each other as people. Not just mother and child. Friends.

Maybe that's what God the Father had in mind all the time. Through growth and maturity, my kids and I are finding a new level of dependence with each other. By doing so will we also find a new level of dependence with God?

Perhaps we'll find it together. Side by side. Truly, that's a dependence we can depend on. No matter what our age.

It Counts

Suppose a man says to God,
"I am guilty but will offend no more.
Teach me what I cannot see;
if I have done wrong, I will not do so again."

JOB 34:31-32

Teenagers live in a hurricane. Sometimes I feel like boarding up the windows and taking cover. Don't they long for a moment of calm? A refuge from the storm that whirls around them? We give them nice things, opportunities, love. But it doesn't seem to matter. They live in chaos. In fact, they seem to thrive in it.

When their chaos overflows into their bedrooms, I get an attitude. It's not even the mess that bothers me as much as what the mess symbolizes: lack of respect.

So I plead. I cajole. I yell. And yet their rooms look as if they are in the middle of an extensive inventory or getting ready for a flea market. But somehow I can't give up. I have to try one more time to reach into their storm....

Carson and Laurel sat on the floor in front of me, their long legs vying for space. I prepared for the ninetieth repetition of the Clean Room Talk. But this time, I felt a different emphasis brewing. The kids were older now—Emily wasn't even around. She was off at college. The essence of the Clean Room Talk needed to go beyond picking up dirty socks.

I took a deep breath and began. "What do your messy rooms tell me?"

The kids exchanged a look. It sounded like a trick question.

I gave them a hint. "It has something to do with respect."

Carson perked up. "When we keep our rooms a mess it shows we don't respect them."

"Or the things in them, or us as your parents, or yourselves."

"Wow," Laurel said. "All that because we don't hang up our clothes?"

"All that," I said. "I want you to go off by yourselves and figure out how you want to handle it. Through the years we've tried everything. My rules haven't worked. So now it's your turn. What will entice you to keep your rooms clean? Reward or punishment, it's up to you."

They looked at me as if I were crazy, but left the room. Maybe I was crazy—or lazy. Truth was, I was weary of trying to come up with "the answer." Charts, star stickers, pop inspections ... years worth of aborted attempts to attain "clean" for more than an hour.

A few minutes later, they returned. Carson was spokesman. "If we keep our rooms clean for a month, we each get $15. If we lie about it, or don't do it, we lose the TV for one week. And if we don't do it three times in a month, we lose all chance of getting the $15."

I said my own internal, "Wow." The conditions were stricter than I would have imposed.

"I agree," I said. "Now go to it. Get them clean."

A while later, they appeared before me. "We're done," they said. Stupid me, I believed them. Only later in the evening did I discover what all mothers discover: that our idea of clean is not our children's idea of clean. It wasn't even close. But after pointing out that dirty clothes do not belong *in* drawers or *under* beds and that the perimeter of the room doesn't have to look like a display at a garage sale, they got back to work. Their discouragement showed.

I showed some mercy. "Since we haven't really gotten started with your deal, we'll say it doesn't count. I'll lessen the penalty. No TV tonight. But you can watch it tomorrow."

Carson shook his head. "No. It *does* count. We lied. We didn't do what we should have done. It counts."

Laurel looked at her brother, appalled. I looked at him, amazed. Somehow in the fifteen years of his life, he had found integrity and honor. He was willing to accept his punishment as deserved and just. He was willing to change. What more can a mother—or God—ask?

In spite of the messy rooms—perhaps because of them—Carson and I experienced a wonderful new emotion. Respect. Toward each other, and toward ourselves.

It's true that teenage chaos gives me an attitude. Yet there is hope. In the hurricane of every teenager there *is* an eye to their whirling, stormy lives. A place of calm, understanding, and even virtue. If only we can find it.

Growing, Growing, Gone

Fathers, do not exasperate your children;
instead, bring them up in the training and
instruction of the Lord.

EPHESIANS 6:4

My little boy is six feet tall—and growing.

My little girl bought her own car.

My littlest girl—who used to sit *next* to me in the recliner—sits alone (though we can still squeeze in if we angle ourselves sideways).

My children are leaving me behind and I don't like it. Don't they know I'm not ready for them to know the facts of life, hold down a job, and say no to me?

That last one is the hardest to take. Having them say no. Although they've never been shy about voicing their opinions since we cracked open the first jar of baby food (pears, no peas) they've been respectful children who did what they were told. Generally. But now—although they're still good kids—they have the audacity to tell me I'm wrong about things. Mothers don't like to hear that. It upsets our maternal equilibrium and brings on feelings of inadequacy (being old enough to have teenagers does that all by itself, thank you very much).

The realization they were growing away from me came after an argument regarding long-sleeved T-shirts. Hardly the typical cause of a World War III escalation, but fourteen-year-old Carson and I did our best to exaggerate the trivial into a battle as to who could be most stubborn, arrogant, and annoying (I think I won).

I had purchased two striped, long-sleeved T-shirts for Carson. I'd used my wealth of knowledge concerning his likes and dislikes. No collars. No buttons. No stupid sayings and only a select few sports teams emblazoned on his shirts. He wore sweatshirts and T-shirts. Period. It seemed logical with winter coming on for him to expand his wardrobe to wear *long-sleeved* T-shirts.

No way.

"I don't like them."

I held the shirt against the striped tee he was wearing. It was a second cousin except for the ten extra inches of sleeve. "It's the same style," I said. "Nearly the same stripe."

He shook his head. "I don't like long sleeves."

"You wear long-sleeved sweatshirts all the time."

"That's different."

Sisters Emily and Laurel fled the room for safer ground. The argument that ensued had nothing to do with logic but had a lot to do with a growing son and a mother who was losing her little boy. Carson had always been the compliant one, the sensitive one. How dare he—

Mark interrupted as I was on the verge of calling in the fashion police for a consultation. "There comes a time when Carson has the right to choose his own clothes," he said (voicing a distasteful amount of truth).

But he's my little boy!

As it was two against one, I surrendered the argument with an appropriate show of martyrdom. I went off to pout. Alone. *My kids didn't need me? Then I didn't need—*

But I *did* need them. I needed to be needed. I needed to have them ask me for help with their homework. I needed them to give me a hug before bed. I needed to chauffeur them to

Girl Scouts or to a friend's house.

But things were changing. Their homework had exceeded my immediate knowledge of Abraham Lincoln and multiplication tables. Having youthful energy (remember that?), the kids stayed up past *my* bedtime. And one of them (soon two of them) could drive themselves anywhere they pleased.

I wanted to hug them tight. Keep them little. Keep them children. Keep them mine.

But they weren't mine anymore. They were themselves. I grieved the loss of the children they once were. Patent leather Mary Janes, Richard Scarry books, and Kool-Aid had surrendered to combat boots, scary books, and Mountain Dew. "Mommy" had succumbed to "Mom." Each day they gained confidence and experience to take them out on their own.

Away from me.

The next day, as I returned the long-sleeved T-shirts to the store, I resisted buying another shirt I thought Carson might like. *I* liked it. But that didn't mean he would like it. I put it back on the rack.

It *was* time he made his own choices. About a lot of things ...

One by one our kids are stepping up to the door of adulthood. They're knocking. It's our choice whether we want to bar the door—or open it, step aside, and let them in.

Welcome.

part 3

Relatives and Other Strangers

*Fellowship, dictatorship,
and showmanship.*

The Blessing Habit

Whoever invokes a blessing in the land
will do so by the God of truth.

ISAIAH 65:16

The checkout lanes were three deep. I jockeyed for position, craning my neck toward the next aisle to see which people in line were waiting to buy just a bottle of shampoo and a birthday card and which were standing behind a cart heaped with Rubbermaid, disposable diapers, and a year's supply of chip dips, wing dings, and sugar wees.

Apparently, there was a run on Rubbermaid, disposable diapers, and sugar wees. It didn't look good.

I took a deep breath, glanced over my own cart and chastised myself. *"He who is without sin, cast the first ..."* My cart was full to overflowing. With a family of five, it seems I can't go into the local discount store without filling my cart with white socks, batteries, kitty litter, toilet paper ...

I turned into the nearest lane and prepared to let my mind drift into La-La Land—that place I visit while waiting in heavy traffic, drive-though lanes, and those return counters where it takes forty-five minutes to exchange the coffee maker that doesn't like to make coffee for one that does.

The gates of La-La Land opened. My eyes started to glaze. My breathing began its descent into catatonia—

"Is this coloring book for you?"

I cleared my head and looked toward the voice, hoping it wasn't talking to me.

A toddler two carts ahead, clutching a new box of jumbo crayons, nodded at the clerk, her face full of pride.

"Cinderella's my favorite, too," said the clerk, a woman who barely came up to my shoulders. "I used to make her dress a different color on every page."

The little girl handed over the box of crayons. The mother paid. Then the clerk put the coloring book and crayons in a separate sack from the mother's purchases and gave it to the little girl. The toddler beamed as if she'd been handed her biggest wish.

I banished La-La Land into oblivion and turned my attention to the clerk as she handled the next person in line. A smile. A personal word. Instead of being bored by the wait, I found myself looking forward to my time as the recipient of the clerk's kind attention.

Finally, it was my turn.

"Cats are wonderful creatures, aren't they?" she said, pulling my giant-sized bag of kitty litter over the scanner. Thus began our short discussion about the attributes of the feline persuasion. When I paid with my credit card, the clerk took a moment to look at the name and said, "Thank you, Mrs. Moser. Have a great day."

I looked at her name tag, a little embarrassed I hadn't taken the time to notice *her* name. "You, too, Iris."

As I loaded the kitty litter into the trunk of my car, I found myself smiling. But the smile wasn't mine. It belonged to Iris.

When I got in the car, three words forced themselves out of my mouth: "Bless her, Lord." I had not planned to say the words. They surfaced from deep inside me; unbidden, yet utterly sincere. I glanced back at the store and could imagine the hand of God reaching down from heaven to pat Iris on the shoulder. And *I* felt blessed.

That was the beginning of a new habit, the blessing habit. Once or twice a day since, it happens with the same suddenness as it did the first time. I'll see a child waiting for the school bus; I'll notice a lone golfer practicing his swing; I'll spot a fellow driver rubbing his forehead; I'll see an elderly man reading the newspaper at the library, the paper raised to within inches of his face ... and those three special words will emerge in my consciousness.

"Bless them, Lord."

And I know he does. And I know it makes a difference. To them—and to me.

Staying Out of the Way

He who trusts in himself is a fool,
but he who walks in wisdom is kept safe.

PROVERBS 28:26

"Don't help!"

Mark stopped dusting the furniture. For a brief moment he looked like a child, his lower lip jutting outwards, his eyebrows raised.

"I was just trying to—"

"I know," I said, holding out my hand, wanting him to relinquish the dust cloth. "And I appreciate the good intentions. But we've got company coming in an hour and there's a certain *way* to dust." I held the dust cloth by the tiniest corner. It looked like a reunion of wax-coated dust bunnies. "You have to use a different cloth on the knickknacks. The furniture polish makes them look ... it's complicated," I said, ignoring the fact that Mark's IQ nearly matches his weight.

He shoved his hands in his pockets. "You could show me."

The clock on the mantel echoed in my ears. Each tick meant less time for tock. "Another day," I said. "When we have more time. As it is, I can do it faster myself."

He stepped aside as I moved to the kitchen to get two clean cloths. Fourteen-year-old Carson met us there. "Can I get out the stuff for the relish tray?" he asked. "I promise I won't eat all the olives."

"No!" I snapped. "I want to arrange the radishes in a special way, I want—"

He also stuffed his hands in his pockets, making the two men in my life look like a set of bookends (one slightly taller, and one slightly slimmer, than the other). Their furrowed foreheads were a perfect match.

"So what can we do to help?" Mark asked.

"Stay out of my way." As the last syllable floundered in the air between us, I yearned to take the words back. I had just proclaimed myself a wicked dictator of last-minute-itis.

They slunk from the room, eager to escape my bark and bite. I shoved my guilt aside as I tackled the dusting. I found little comfort in the fact that I was doing it "right." After finishing the coffee table, I glanced around, hoping Carson and Mark would show themselves so I could apologize. "I'm sorry, guys. I didn't mean to jump on you. It's just that—"

Suddenly, I found myself mentally repeating the phrase to someone else... *I'm sorry, God. I didn't mean to jump on them. It's just that they got in the way. If only they'd let me handle things, I could—*

I stopped my dusting. I wondered how many times God had thought those same thoughts—about me? How many times had he suffered my good intentions? How many times had *my* way gotten in the way of *his* way?

Often.

Yet God had been very patient with me. He'd never brushed me off, telling me he didn't have time to teach me his way. And even though he was capable of doing *everything* himself, he never did, being eternally patient until I learned that his way was best.

Following the sound of the television, I walked to the family room. I found the men waiting (hiding out is a better term).

I cleared my throat. "Carson? I guess I do need your help with the relish tray."

"But what about the radishes?"

"I'll show you how I want them arranged."

"But the time ..." Mark said, tapping his watch.

"The guests will understand. And I could use your help with the dusting."

Mark gave me that much-too-knowledgeable look he had honed to perfection. "Are you sure we won't be in the way?"

"We'll work on it," I said.

And we did. With God's help, we did.

Egos at Fifty Paces

I wish that all men were as I am. But each man has his own gift from God; one has this gift, another has that.

1 CORINTHIANS 7:7

Opposites attract—and often stick. I know. For the past twenty-two years Mark and I have attracted, distracted, and counteracted each other.

We don't like the same things. He likes roller coasters. The drop of the escalator at the mall is thrill enough for me. He likes hot weather. I don't *do* summer. He likes movies with car chases and special effects. I prefer boy-girl chases and romantic finesse.

While we were dating we had no idea our tastes were so diverse. Adhering to proper dating etiquette, we molded our individual preferences to the other's desires. I pretended to like baseball and Mark teased me into thinking he craved doing the Hustle like John Travolta. With innocent accommodation, I tried smothered steak and he tried creamed tuna on toast. I tried to watch golf (it was a good chance to nap) and he tried to watch figure skating (he *did* like the short skirts).

It was done with the best of intentions but with mixed results—I learned to like smothered steak and he learned to tolerate creamed tuna on toast. When we became engaged we let a few of our true opinions loose. But not a lot. Our main goal was to please our partner.

With marriage came reality. Relentlessly, it pushed gaga love off its pedestal and peppered it with utility bills and shared chores. Reality let Mark discover that my hair has a natural tendency to turn out when it's supposed to turn in. Reality let me witness his favorite sweatpants in all their hole-i-ness. Reality let us realize that on our budget, macaroni and cheese was not a side dish, it was an entrée.

As the newlywed manners wore off, self-pity moved in like a pesky relative. We'd make valiant efforts to kick it out only to have it sneak in the back door, lugging with it doubt and frustration. For all Mark's good qualities—and there were many—I wondered why God hadn't matched me with a man who yearned to dance the night away as he crooned Johnny Mathis tunes in my ear. And Mark had to wonder why he hadn't been paired with a woman who reveled in outdoor activities during the scorching summer.

Occasionally, logic seized control, making us see the advantages of our differences. I never had to worry about Mark snarfing down the rocky road ice cream, and he never had to worry about me taking a single bite of his vanilla—unless it was drowning in hot fudge. He could never accuse me of losing his Queen album, and my John Denver cassette was entirely my own.

Yet as ego matched ego, we clung to the underlying conviction that "my way is better than yours." We held onto the belief that the characteristics that made each of us unique were our "identities," while the characteristics that made our spouse unique were merely "quirks." Big heads and large shoulder chips prevailed. We chose to forget what Scripture thought of such matters: "'Let him who boasts boast in the Lord.' For it is not the one who commends himself who is approved, but the one whom the Lord commends" (2 Corinthians 10:17-18).

When our three children were little, they were the objects of our tug of war. *You will like baseball. No, ballet! We'll spend our vacation at the lake. No, the mountains!* Poor babies, no wonder they have such long arms. Yet it was their influence that helped us bury our egos in an unmarked grave.

When the kids got old enough to have an opinion, we discovered that Emily loved the stomach-wrenchings of roller coasters, Carson thrilled to the crack of ball against bat, and Laurel didn't move across a room without marking a beat. Emily liked angel food, Carson liked chocolate, and Laurel liked broccoli (a true individualist). But instead of thinking of them as being "wrong," we found these vast differences in our children refreshing. Exciting.

If we accepted the differences in our children, why couldn't we accept the differences in each other? The apostle Peter said, "Love each other deeply, because love covers over a multitude of sins" (1 Peter 4:8). The sins we had. But what about the depth of our love? Was there a way to find sweet fruit in our sour grapes?

The first step was to put away our weapons—our egos. When we stopped fighting the ways we were different we suddenly saw how our varied interests added to the diversity of our lives. Because of me, Mark experienced Mozart, Sondheim, and Gershwin. And because of him, I learned the nuances of a curve ball, a bunt, and cotton candy. In 1 Corinthians 12:4-6 we read: "There are different kinds of gifts, but the same Spirit. There are different kinds of service, but the same Lord. There are different kinds of working, but the same God works all of them in all men." Neither talent or interest was better than the other. God could use both of us in a unique way. And he did. *Because* Mark and I have different talents and interests, our children have enjoyed a vast breadth of experiences.

In addition, when we kept our egos in check we noticed how our strengths balanced each other's weaknesses; our pros offset each other's cons. My energy balanced Mark's procrastination. His deliberate ways balanced my gusts of impulsiveness. His stubbornness ... matched mine.

It was all a matter of perspective, of copping the right attitude. The key was to move beyond the natural inclination to compete and remember we were on the same team.

We don't sweat the differences anymore, although I still prefer *Sense and Sensibility* to *Twister*. We know these differences exist for a purpose. Along with our love, God has given us unique gifts, identities, and qualities to share. It would be shameful not to use them, appreciate them. With time we've learned to "be at peace with each other" (Mark 9:50).

Our differences don't take away from our life together, they add to it. The sum of our lives makes a better whole. A whole marriage.

A Sonata in Me-Major

We have different gifts, according to the grace given us.

ROMANS 12:6

Some people are so talented it makes me wonder if I was indisposed when God handed out his special gifts. Was I napping? Distracted with making my computer behave? Or worse, was I in the restroom helping my kids negotiate the intricacies of the soap dispenser?

Did I miss it when God stood before humankind and asked for volunteers?

"Who wants the gift of patience to work with teenagers, toddlers, and tired husbands?"

"Who wants the gift of generosity to give of their time, talents, and treasures with nary a grumble?"

"Who wants the gift of energy so they'll never need a ten-minute nap and actually look forward to entertaining twenty-one relatives at Thanksgiving?"

Don't look at me.

I'd love to have these talents. If God had given them to me I'm sure I would be very pleased with myself. He has to forgive me if I look on the recipients of such gifts with a large dose of envy. My pitiful levels of patience, generosity, and energy are proof that God also doles out booby prizes. Truth is, I'm jealous.

This jealousy is not becoming and often leads to the competitive side of me keeping score. I secretly rig the unofficial contest of who has the most gifts so I have a fighting chance to at least call it a tie. It took the exhibit of an extraordinary talent to make me find a more godly response....

At our church there is a teenage boy who is a music prodigy. When our regular organist is on vacation in the summer, Colin fills in. Expertly. On this particular summer Sunday, Colin played a sonata *he* had written. I sat in awe of his talents. How had he tapped into the notes, the rhythm, the inspiration? The congregation burst into appreciative applause. When Pastor Tom moved to the pulpit he shook his head in wonder and said, "Seeing someone use his potential to such a high level inspires me to look at my own talents. What can I do better?"

Where was his jealousy? For if ever there was a reason to be jealous, it would have been because of Colin's extraordinary talent.

I listened to Pastor Tom's remarks, and found them hitting the bull's eye of my own envious heart. I asked myself how I could better use the gifts God had given me. It wasn't a matter of looking *at* myself, it involved looking *inside* myself to see how I could use my gifts for the benefit of others—not just for my own selfish gratification and certainly not to win an I've-got-more-than-you contest. I needed to raise my hand and volunteer my gifts instead of hoarding them for myself.

I also needed to recognize attributes in other people. What gifts did I see in my kids? My spouse? My neighbors? Did I appreciate their gifts as I wanted them to appreciate mine?

What would happen if we all used our gifts to a higher level until we inspired other people to use their gifts to a higher level... and on and on?

Wow!

Maybe I *was* present when God handed out his gifts. I simply have to look deeper, bring them to the surface, utilize them until I'm playing my own sonata. I need to tap into the notes, the rhythm, and the inspiration that are mine to share.

I need to tap into the giver of my gifts. I need to tap into God.

Shh! I think I hear some heavenly applause.

Being There

For you have delivered me from death
and my feet from stumbling,
that I may walk before God
in the light of life.

PSALM 56:13

"I have cancer," my mother said over the phone.

I fell into stunned silence. Then a burst of anger. I wanted to slam the phone into its cradle, over and over, until it shattered into a pile of jagged pieces. It was the phone's fault. It had to be.

It had to be somebody's fault.

I took a deep breath to steady my voice. "What are you going to—"

"I'm going to have surgery. Next week. Two days after Christmas." Her voice grabbed at the last word, asking the question that shot like a bolt of lightning through the phone line between us.

Would this Christmas be her last?

"Can't you have some other kind of treatment?" I asked. "Do they *have* to do surgery?"

Mom's voice was matter-of-fact, not at all like my emotional whimper. "They could do a lesser surgery," she said, "but then I'd have to go through chemotherapy. This is the best chance to get it all. The doctor explained to me what—"

I stopped listening. *Please, Lord, not my mother. She's constant. She's always been there. She'll always—*

I'd never thought about my parents dying. I knew that was the proper order of things, the oldest generation moving on, making way for the next. But it was always a dim thought for the future. Not now. *Not my mother.*

"—planned it for the twenty-seventh so you girls could stick around after Christmas and be here."

I came back to reality. "Of course we'll be there. I'll stay as long as you want." My mind swam with logistics. "We can drive two cars up for Christmas and Mark can take the kids home with him. I'm sure Crystie and Lois will stay too. And Tom's in town. We'll all be there for you."

"I'd appreciate that," she said.

It was the least we could do.

The most we could do was pray. And pray. And pray.

But what to pray? How to pray? I'd have to trust God to lead me. "Lord, help my mother. Help all of us. We need you...."

❧

I tiptoed into the hospital room with my sisters, Lois and Crystie. Dad was there at the bedside, holding Mom's hand. Stroking it. Mom's face was pale, her eyes closed. The pillow that held her head seemed to have more substance than she did. The lights were dim, softening the images. An IV was taped to her hand. The only sound was the beep-beep of a monitor.

Dad saw us. His smile struggled against the sagging face of worry.

"The doctor said it went well. But she's still fading in and out."

Mom opened an eye at the sound of his voice. She attempted a smile meant just for him. I took her other hand. So soft. So fragile. She turned toward us.

"You're here," she said.

"We're here."

"*I'm* here," she said. Her eyes closed. She forced them open. "The first thing I did when I woke up was thank God for letting me get through it."

Amen.

∿

"How do you like my new pajamas?" Mom asked when we came to visit the next morning.

The jade silk was a big improvement over the flimsy white hospital gown.

"You look lovely." And she did. Her cheeks were rosy. Her hair combed. Her face smiling.

"Did you find the leftover turkey and the cranberry salad I left for you in the refrigerator?" she asked, ever the hostess. "And in the pantry, did you find the bread I baked?"

"I bet you offered the doctor a cup of coffee during surgery, didn't you?" I said.

Our laughter tinkled like music. We admired the flowers and cards brought by thoughtful friends and family. We admired Mom. Positive, confident. An amazing woman.

She sat a bit straighter for her next announcement. "I get to go home tomorrow."

"So soon?"

She squeezed Dad's ever-present hand. "There's nothing more they can do for me here. It's done. Now I have to recover. I want to go home."

Crystie asked the question we needed to ask. "When will they know the results of the pathology report?"

"Tomorrow," Mom said.

Another day.

We cleaned the house for Mom's homecoming. I organized the pantry (does anyone really need five bottles of soy sauce?). Lois cleaned out the refrigerator, a chore which involved throwing away the contents of a dozen containers holding ancient dabs of this and that. Crystie made casseroles to take Mom and Dad through the next few days. We kidded about making the ultimate casserole by combining all the dabs from the fridge. Noodle-Jell-O Surprise.

Then we left for home, letting the actual homecoming be a private affair for two. Our goodbye hugs exposed our relief—and our fears that it wasn't over.

"Call us as soon as you know," we instructed Dad.

As we turned our vehicles toward home—heading west, east, and south—I could almost see the prayers rising through the cars toward heaven.

"Thank you, God, for taking care of her. Keep her safe. Make her healthy again."

"The cancer is gone," said my mother. "The doctor says they got it all. I'm going to be all right."

I wanted to kiss the phone. Cradle it. Sing its praises for giving me the good news.

But there was someone else to praise. Someone who had been there through it all, heard our prayers—and answered them gloriously.

I fell to my knees.

Missing the Chance

But a Samaritan, as he traveled, came where the man was; and when he saw him, he took pity on him.

LUKE 10:33

The evening clouds billowed higher as if they were contemplating a storm. Rain would be welcome as the ninety-degree temperatures sucked the moisture from all living things—me included. I shut the pages of the book I was reading while sprawled on a chaise lounge and gave my attention to the sky. So perfect. So beautiful.

I found myself praying. Praising. *Thank you for all you give me, Lord. Use me. Let me help you by giving something back.*

I rarely take walks in the evening. I am a morning person and take my walks in the early A.M. before most of the world is awake (including myself, if I'm totally honest). But that night the clouds and the pink of the sunset called to me.

I laced up my walking shoes and clipped on my Walkman. And though I *always* head north, on this night, I headed south—to better see the sunset in the west. Or so I thought.

After three blocks I neared the bottom of the hill where Hayes intersects 141ST. There, I saw a man on the corner across the street, holding a piece of paper. It was dusk and his features were hazy but I could see he was wearing white tennis shorts and a white polo shirt. He looked at me. Did he say something?

I ignored my plan to turn right and turned left to cross the street toward him. I nudged my headphones off my ears so I could hear him if he *was* saying something. I said, "Hello" to cover my curiosity with normal courtesy.

"Is this Hayes?" he asked, pointing up the street from where I'd come.

Ah, so that's it, he wants directions.

"That's Hayes," I said, continuing to walk, but turning toward him as I passed.

The man folded the paper, mumbling. "I'm legally blind and I'm trying to find my son. I can't see the street signs."

I nodded. I repeated, "Yes, that's Hayes" and continued on my walk.

After a half-block, I stopped and looked back. *What am I doing? A man who is legally blind asks for my help and I point him in the right direction and leave him to it?*

With a sudden urgency, I backtracked, turning north on Hayes, hoping to catch up with him and be available if he needed more help. With my half-block diversion, he should have been a block ahead of me.

The sunset was past its prime, the shadows closing in. I shut off the Walkman, feeling the need to concentrate in my efforts to find him, to right the wrong I'd done.

There he is, up to the left. A few more steps revealed my "man" was a white mailbox. I quickened my pace. He shouldn't be so far ahead....

I heard some boys playing basketball in a driveway. His son? I hurried toward the sound, hoping to see the father waiting for the last few baskets before heading home. My guilt would be relieved.

Five boys. No adults. *He wasn't there.*

My throat tightened. Tears threatened. *Oh, Lord. I'm so sorry.*

Why didn't I stop and offer to help him? Why did I selfishly keep walking? I searched the street ahead, hoping to spot the glow of the white shorts and shirt as he wandered in the dark. *Please, God. If he still needs help, let me find him. Give me another chance to help. Please forgive me.*

Too soon I was home. I stopped in my driveway and scanned the street. Right and left. Up and down. There was no man. He had disappeared as if … as if he'd never existed.

I sat on the front steps a long time. Watching for the man. Praying for the man. And praying for myself. An hour earlier I'd asked God to use me. Within minutes, he'd answered my prayer. And within minutes, I'd let him down.

As the clouds rumbled in the distance, promising relief from summer's burden of heat, I asked God for relief from my own personal burden of guilt.

I asked him for—and by his mercy received—another chance.

Trusting the Milkman

The Lord watches over you—
the Lord is your shade at your right hand;
the sun will not harm you by day,
nor the moon by night.

PSALM 121:5-6

Slipping on my bunny slippers, I toddled into the quiet living room to—

The bunny slippers should tell you I'm not talking recent history here. They don't make such things to fit my size ten feet, or if they do, I certainly wouldn't wear them and risk being disowned by my family. And as far as toddling goes … people might say, "She bounded into the room." She "stormed." She "tripped." But never "toddled." Not since my much smaller feet dangled from a chair.

Anyway, back to my story. Slipping on my bunny slippers, I toddled into the quiet living room to play with Colorforms and Tiny Tears. There was something special about the house full of family and yet silent (perhaps that's why I still get up at 5:00 A.M.).

Once a week, when I was playing quietly in the living room, I'd hear the kitchen door. I'd hear the soft thud of adult feet across the linoleum. I'd hear the refrigerator open. A clink of glass against glass. Then retreating footsteps and the soft click of the door. Sometimes I continued playing but sometimes I ventured toward the sound and peeked around the corner.

Was it a burglar? If so, the burglar was wearing a white uniform and cap. If so, the burglar waved at me and smiled.

It was no burglar. It was the milkman.

Looking back on the phenomenon, I marvel at this astounding example of trust. Instead of waking us on his early morning rounds, the Skyline Dairy milkman entered our unlocked kitchen, checked our refrigerator, and determined what dairy products we needed. I can't imagine experiencing such an act of trust today.

What has happened to us in the decades since I was four?

Now, when I'm home alone writing, I keep the doors locked. When I drive my daughter to school I close the garage door for the five minutes I'm gone. When we go to church we lock the car doors in the parking lot thirty feet from the front door. *If* we had a milkman who made house calls (even doctors don't make house calls), I would never consider letting him into the house on his own, especially when my family was sleeping. And never when there'd be a chance one of my kids would be up, alone, and vulnerable to all the nasty possibilities that flash through our minds on a regular basis. This is how we deal with daily life, living in our relatively crime-free neighborhood.

What's gotten into us?

Fear has gotten into us. Even if I resolved to be more trusting, to keep my doors unlocked, to let my youngest child wander the mall by herself, and not to be suspicious of strange cars trolling the neighborhood, I couldn't do it. I shouldn't do it. It wouldn't be wise. Just because I trust doesn't mean the world deserves my trust. If the milkman had betrayed our confidence, the bond would have been broken—irreparably.

Over the years too many bonds have been broken. To ignore the safety precautions of locked doors and being wary of strangers would be like riding in a roller coaster with no seat belt or safety bar. It would require nerves of steel and an addled mind.

So what's the answer? How can we learn to trust again?

We have to learn *whom* to trust again. There is only one who is worthy of our trust, who won't let us down, who considers our best interests at all times. God. Man has changed. For the worse? Maybe. But God hasn't changed. He is still here for us and will be here for us. "For great is his love toward us, and the faithfulness of the Lord endures forever. Praise the Lord" (Psalm 117).

Amen.

Brother, Can You Spare a Dime?

As we have opportunity, let us do good to all people.
GALATIANS 6:10

It was only a dime. Ten cents. Not enough to make a difference in the world.

Or was it?

I was in the checkout lane at a drug store, my cart full of the necessities of life: shampoo, paper towels, Diet Coke, Butterfinger bars. Two adolescent boys were ahead of me. The clerk was holding out her hand. The boys were desperately excavating the contents of their pockets.

Two Jolly Ranchers, a bent stick of Juicy Fruit, a lint sculpture, and a house key.

The clerk rolled her eyes. "You need another dime."

The cheeks of the boys reddened to a shade resembling "Babycakes Blush" that I'd seen in the makeup aisle.

I opened my purse and dug out a dime.

"Here, this will take care of it."

The clerk looked relieved. The boys looked embarrassed. The pen that had been the cause of the commotion was placed in a sack.

None of us met each other's eyes until the boys retreated a step toward the door. Then the owner of the new pen turned to me, smiled sheepishly, and said, "Thanks."

I felt as if I'd won an Oscar. I lived off that tiny bit of kindness for the rest of the day. I know it sounds absurd. But at the time, it didn't matter that in the scheme of the world's problems, my giving two boys a dime didn't mean a whit. It didn't.

And yet it did.

Maybe those boys will remember the lady with the shampoo and the Butterfingers. Maybe they will help someone else. Maybe they'll do something monumental like solve world hunger or bring about worldwide peace....

I'm getting carried away. Maybe they'll simply be nice to someone else and the chain will continue.

Maybe that is enough.

Guard Your Heart

Finally, brothers, whatever is true, whatever is noble, whatever is right, whatever is pure, whatever is lovely, whatever is admirable—if anything is excellent or praiseworthy—think about such things.

PHILIPPIANS 4:8

I'm a wimp. Blood, cuss words, violence. If one of my kids scrapes a knee, I can do my motherly duty, but if it needs stitches, I call in stronger stomachs. I know that words are merely puffs of air and yet when I hear a cuss word, it's like a needle in my heart. And movies … I have a vivid imagination. I don't need to see the details to get the gist of what's going on.

Which is my point. In today's world there are times when we are confronted with sights and sounds that are offensive. We all know how to *avoid* such intrusions: don't watch the TV show, don't read the book, don't listen to the comedian, lock yourself in a closet. But it's not always that easy. Sometimes we find ourselves in situations where we have to deal with the distasteful. What do we do then to "guard our hearts"?

An example: as a writer I go to seminars and classes to gather information that will enhance my work. At one such talk, a county medical examiner had been invited to explain the amazing advances in scientific pathology.

Perhaps I was naive. Perhaps I expected a Quincy-character to speak to us; to explain in a fatherly, soft voice how forensics let the dead speak.

I was so wrong.

There were slides. We arranged our chairs so we could see the screen. The first slides were educational. Lists. Words. Details. But the next ones ...

My eyes were shocked to see a vivid slide of a man who'd died in a hit-and-run. I quickly looked in my lap.

I can't see this. I pretended to take copious notes.

Surely, the speaker would flip through such slides; realize what was normal for him was horrifying to the rest of us.

But he didn't. In fact, he seemed to take special pleasure in showing examples of his "patients." He joked. He teased. He acted as if these people were as inconsequential as a box of paper clips or a coffee mug.

These people were somebody's son, somebody's wife.

I looked toward the exit. With misguided enthusiasm, I'd positioned myself front and center. In the cramped room I'd have to weave my way through the entire audience to leave. I couldn't listen. I couldn't look. I couldn't escape.

My hand started writing. "Guard your heart ... guard your heart. 'Above all else, guard your heart, for it is the wellspring of life'" (Proverbs 4:23).

"... **now** this man was stabbed fifty-two times ..."

Good thoughts. I need good thoughts. *Mark. The kids, Emily, Carson, Laurel. My brother's wedding the previous weekend.*

"... you can see there were two different knives used ..."

How beautiful it had been when they were married in the garden, the sun miraculously appearing after days and days of rain.

"... one brother accused the other brother of doing the killing but we found ..."

The glow of happiness on my brother's face. The fun of singing around the piano at the reception.

I glanced at the people closest to me to see if they were fighting the same battle against this brutal reality. Other eyes met mine and looked to their laps. I was not alone.

"This one looks like he's asleep, doesn't he?"

Sleeping in the living room at my parents' home, the house full to overflowing with wedding guests. The sounds of Mom clattering in the kitchen making a breakfast casserole at 5:00 A.M. The joy of holding my sister-in-law's twin nieces, so innocent as they slept through the laughter and hum of wedding voices....

Finally another voice. "I'm afraid that's all the time we have tonight. Perhaps our speaker will consent to come back and finish his presentation."

A few people murmured their enthusiasm. Most remained silent.

When I reached my car, I felt drained. The tears started. I let them flow, knowing they were more important than any complacency and professional detachment. I cried for the evil in the world. I cried for the need for autopsies and medical examiners.

And I cried for the "patients."

Putting Things Together

My heart took delight in all my work,
and this was the reward for all my labor.

ECCLESIASTES 2:10

People are hesitant to try new things. When color televisions first came out they were rare—and expensive. Our neighbors down the street were among the first to take a chance, and as such were revered by the neighborhood kids and hated by our parents. On many Sunday nights my friends and I would gather in their basement to watch one of the few color shows in existence: Walt Disney's "The Wonderful World of Color." We piled in front of the screen to gawk as the NBC peacock unfurled its cartoon feathers—in living color. What a thrill.

When it came time for our family to get a color TV my father hesitated. As with any new invention the price was high and the quality uneven. He decided the best course of action was to make our own—from a kit. The extent of most people's experience with kits is to make a plastic airplane or a needlepoint pillow. Not my dad. He was an engineer and held the belief (however false) that people were logical animals and—if only they were organized and patient—they could accomplish most anything. I've spent my life trying *not* to prove him wrong.

When the kit for the color TV arrived, we carried it down to his basement shop. I helped Dad separate all the parts. ("Preparation is essential, Nancy.") Every evening we would assemble a small component of the television. Circuit boards, tubes, wires … at various times we were instructed to test a unit. The tension mounted. Would it work? Would we have to start over? Step by step, part by part, our persistence was rewarded.

Throughout our lives, there was never a question of *if* we could do things. The lesson of Mom and Dad's do-it-yourself philosophy stuck. When I wanted a down sleeping bag and a down coat, I sewed them from a kit. When I wanted a new light fixture, I took down the old and wired in the new (I even remembered to turn off the electricity first). When the innards of the toilet stopped working, I bought new ones and put them in with nary a drip on the floor.

However, not being the meticulous engineer that my father was, my methods were often beyond the instructions in any how-to book. They veered toward the ingenious. (This is my word—other people's descriptions are less generous.) When I installed ceramic tile on the wall between our kitchen counter and cupboards, in order to get the grout into the corners and in order to work at such an awkward angle, I used my hand as a trowel. I dipped my fingers in the oozy grout and slopped it on. (Helpful hint: grout has a tendency to make the skin dry up like mud in the desert—must have something to do with the lime.)

Dad—and eventually Mark—*used* to cringe. Now they've learned to stay away until after my project is completed. The finished product is easier to take than my unprecedented methods.

All this self-sufficiency satisfies. And it definitely has its place in life. I figure if God wanted us to sit and meditate all the time, he would have switched things around and made six days for worship and the seventh for work. Yet sometimes it's hard for tool-woman Nancy to admit that she *can't* do something; that she *can't* fix everything; or that she has to depend on someone else.

It's been a struggle to learn there are two sides to life: facts and faith. Yet submitting to God and subduing a leaky faucet can be compatible. It's like electricity flowing through a light fixture. Neither element is complete without the other. But once they are connected right … life can sizzle.

Colossians 3:17 says, "And whatever you do, whether in word or deed, do it all in the name of the Lord Jesus, giving thanks to God the Father through him." I thank Dad for teaching me how to handle the technical side of things, but I have to thank my other Father for teaching me how to handle the biblical side. There is no conflict between them. Both agree on the philosophy, "Just do it."

Vive la Différence!

Just as each of us has one body with many members, and these members do not all have the same function, so in Christ we who are many form one body, and each member belongs to all the others.

ROMANS 12:4-5

I didn't notice our differences until we stood to sing the first hymn.

The head of the man seated next to me—whose shoulders were in line with mine when we were seated—now came up to my chin.

I slumped self-consciously. If only I hadn't worn my peach heels to church I would have ... still been six inches taller than my most immediate neighbor in the pew.

I'm a tall woman: five-foot-nine in my stocking feet on carpet. Five-ten if you make me stand on a hard floor. This is not some new revelation. I've been this tall since the eighth grade. Sometimes a plus—but often a minus—I've learned to tolerate being a tall woman in a short woman's world.

As we started the second verse of the hymn I noticed a woman two pews up. She made me feel short. She stood next to a man who—if he could dribble a basketball—would be a first round draft pick in the NBA. I stood a little taller.

As the music of the organ and our voices continued to fill the room, I did a further inventory of the congregation. To my right, a man sang with a lustrous bass voice, his jowls trembling with his vibrato. A teen boy stretched the sleeves of his sweater over his hands, his cropped, bleached hair and earring announcing to the world that his taste was generations away from mine. A couple behind me jostled a wriggling toddler, their pleas to shush and be still reminding me of the fractured joys of bringing my own little ones into the sanctuary years ago. An elderly woman with a flowered hat held the hymnal close to her thick glasses, her shrill soprano soaking into the pages.

We were all so different. Tall, short, wide, thin, young, old. When we left the church we'd travel home in vans, pickup trucks, or Cadillacs. For Sunday dinner we'd eat fried chicken, chow mein, steak, or spaghetti. We'd spend the afternoon golfing, reading mysteries, or practicing the drums. We'd go to bed at nine, eleven, or two.

I write. He teaches. She heals. Yet another builds.

Different. And yet the same.

For all of us had made the same choice that morning. We'd come to church. We stood side by side, the height and strength of our shoulders forming a staggered stair-step of humanity. We sang together, flat and sharp, loud and soft. We bowed our heads in prayer. The humble. The urgent.

We opened our hearts, united in a common goal to know the One who made our differences; who understood the whys of it—even if we did not.

Our differences made us special, just as our common goal to worship God made us one.

Holidays Are Relative

Let me get you something to eat, so you can be refreshed and then go on your way—now that you have come to your servant.

GENESIS 18:5

The doorbell rings. As I walk through the living room to answer it, I pick up a cat toy with a bell in it, and put it in my pocket. It jingles as I walk.

"Welcome!" I say, opening the door to the conquering hoard who share the same nose, eyes, temper, and last name.

They blow in with a gust of winter air. Their boots, gloves, and coats fill the entry closet. They come bearing edible gifts. Pumpkin pies, grandma buns, and sugar cookies with sprinkles.

The kids make a beeline for the basement, where all good children live. The men flood into the family room, the women into the kitchen. The lavatory gets a workout. I question the hours spent dusting, cleaning, and polishing. There's little house to see between the luggage and laughing bodies.

"Are you jingling, Nancy?" someone asks.

I retrieve the cat toy and hold it up sheepishly, demonstrating its jingle. The cat looks at me hopefully but I slip the toy into a drawer. Kitten walks away, her tail in the air, as if to tell me she didn't want it anyway.

"Can I offer anyone something to drink?"

So begins the grand opening of the Moser Holiday Inn. For three days it will dispense 53,490 calories, 5,349 grams of fat, and enough diet pop to trick my family into thinking they're being true to their diet. I try to accommodate their unique tastes but find it hard since my kids think yams taste as funny as they sound, and there's always one practicing vegetarian (practicing, meaning they'll eat a Big Mac next week).

There are plenty of hands to help. Too many. Launching the space shuttle takes less coordination than making a meal for sixteen with all this extra help. I'd like to tell them to leave it to me, but I realize helping is a part of holiday bonding.

Sports fans take root in front of the television. They aren't picky. They're fascinated with football, archery, and even Pepsi commercials starring Shaquille O'Neal. The competitive spirits who like to *participate* set up Trivial Pursuit and Hearts in the dining room. The rest of the adults congregate in the kitchen to discuss taxes, college football, the pros and cons of kids, and the recipe for pecan-pumpkin crunch cake. The children remain in the basement. As long as their screams are decibels away from blood-curdling, we leave them alone. An occasional toddler escapes to find Mommy's leg but he's soon back in the basement, bribed by a sugar cookie.

The sleeping arrangements (why am I ready to go to bed by seven?) are imaginative. Although I'd hinted that some people should stay over Wednesday night and some Thursday night, I was misunderstood and everyone is staying both nights. Kids are easy. Toss them a truckload of sleeping bags, put all the decorative couch pillows into pillow cases, and they'll camp on the nearest floor. Every cushioned surface has a designated body.

Eventually the oxygen in the house grows thin from all the hot air that's been exchanged. Fresh air is needed in order to prevent permanent brain damage. Where to go? Groups are formed to go shopping, to the art museum, and to the video store (a request from the basement). In the ceremony called the Juggling of the Cars, I am left out.

"We can fit you in, Nancy, if you sit on Scott's lap," says one.

"I can stay behind and keep you company," offers another.

No.

I sigh, shake my head like a good martyr, and say I'll be all right. I wave goodbye from the porch as the caravan pulls away and spreads over the city like a holiday virus. Back inside, I crack the door to the basement and consider venturing into no-adult-land, just to check. I decide I'm not that dumb—or brave.

I tiptoe into my bedroom and lock the door. Stretching out on the bed, I clasp my arms over my stomach like a peaceful corpse. I close my eyes and take a deep breath.

Silence.

There is a slight thud in the basement. A cat meows from the other side of the door. A toilet flushes from the deepest recess of the house—twice. I resist the urge to check. I am not going to leave my lair until the caravan returns. I will not leave—

I sit up, alert. *I forgot to make the pistachio salad! It's supposed to chill—*

Before I realize what I'm doing I'm mixing pineapple and Jell-O. While the counters are dirty (again) I decide to mix the potato casserole. Then I set the table for another dinner, re-arranging the flowers of the centerpiece.

I put my mental to-do lists on hold and linger over the traditions of the holiday. Does God appreciate our celebration? Does he take joy in our laughter? The running children? The enticing smells wafting from the kitchen? My exhaustion?

He must. Our family is an extension of his family. From oldest grandpa to youngest babe, we are all his children. And he is our Father. We are gathered together because of him.

I hear the caravan pulling into the driveway. Where did the time go?

I straighten a candle and head to the door.

"Welcome back," I say.

And with his blessing, I mean it.

A Harvest of Peace

You will go out in joy
and be led forth in peace;
the mountains and hills
will burst into song before you,
and all the trees of the field
will clap their hands.

ISAIAH 55:12

When I was a child, our family vacations were often spent camping in the mountains of the western United States. My father designed a tent that could comfortably sleep six—as long as nobody snored, giggled, or had to go to the bathroom. He built an ingenious trailer that held the tent, cots, and sleeping bags. It also had built-in dresser drawers for clothes, a pantry, a sink, and storage for the finer things in life. Namely an art box.

Even if we did not tune into our artistic side during the rest of the year, in the course of those few summer weeks we pulled out the paper, the paints, and the colored pencils and created "art."

It was rarely a communal undertaking. One by one, we would procure the art box and walk off into the mountains in search of solitude. There, sitting on a boulder, we would commune with the fluttering of the aspen leaves, the ground squirrels darting between the roots, the music of a rushing stream, and the heady smell of pines that purified the lungs and tickled the nose.

We would get lofty notions into our heads—notions that we had talent. If Monet and Van Gogh could be famous for painting a few water lilies and sunflowers, surely the world would gasp when they witnessed our mountain stream and columbine. A dab here, a swish there … how do artists make the three-dimensional two-dimensional? We found it was harder than it looks.

Yet by dipping our paintbrush into the water and studying a tree that had been a sapling when pioneers first crossed these peaks, we found ourselves one-on-one with creation. We discovered the breadth of our talent wasn't important. We found peace. This peace was the true harvest of our art, for it would last—at least for a little while. When we returned to the commotion of the family, there was a new awareness. Eating pancakes made over a fire, sitting under thousands of stars without the interference of man-made lights, having a cold nose in the morning as we snuggled in our sleeping bags….

The peace of our art in the mountains gave us new eyes to see that *all of this* was very, very good.

Bosom Buddies

*A man of many companions may come to ruin, but
there is a friend who sticks closer than a brother.*

PROVERBS 18:24

True friends are as rare as lightning in a blizzard—and just as
dazzling.

I'm friendly. I can talk to total strangers and make them feel
at home. I can negotiate the proper party mingle and can even
be quite witty with a plate of cheese and crackers in my hand.
But as far as enjoying many deep down bosom-buddy friend-
ships? Only a few have brightened my life.

When I lived in Nebraska I had one particularly good friend,
Katie. She and I met while we were both appearing in the chorus of "Annie" at the community playhouse. Within minutes of
meeting each other we fell into the easy rhythm of lifelong
friends. We listened, we laughed, we gave advice and kept
secrets.

But then, after seven years of friendship, I moved to Kansas.
And I missed her. As she was a worse letter writer than I, we
contented ourselves with a few visits and phone calls. It just
wasn't the same.

One day, feeling rather sorry for myself, I prayed that God
would bless me with another best friend. I knew I was asking a
lot, and I was nearly resigned to having a life full of numerous
acquaintances but few dear *friends* when ... the name "Katie"
popped into my head.

"No, God. Not Katie in Lincoln. A new friend, here in
Kansas."

I didn't think any more about my prayer until two weeks later when I went to a Christian writer's group for the first time. It was a wonderful evening. Their openness and willingness to talk about how they had experienced God working in their lives was true inspiration. After the main meeting, when we sat around drinking iced tea, I found myself next to a woman who had the most beautiful freckled skin and red hair. And when she smiled ... We got along famously, our laughter and camaraderie drawing the envied notice of other members. "You two act as if you've known each other forever." That's what it felt like. Friends forever.

I went home thrilled to have found a new friend. The next day I wrote her a note, taking a risk by exposing my hopes that our friendship would grow and even putting myself on the line further when I recounted my prayer for a best friend. I sent the letter, feeling foolish, vulnerable—and hopeful. Oh, well. If nothing came of it, I wouldn't be any worse off than I was before.

A few days later, she called. My note had made her day. We met for lunch and talked for two and a half hours over pork tenderloins and french fries. To have a friend I could talk to about God and family and writing ... she was truly an answered prayer.

And not so surprisingly, her name was Katy.

Good Morning, Lord

I rise before dawn and cry for help;
I have put my hope in your word.

PSALM 119:147

"Early to bed, early to rise, makes a man healthy, wealthy, and wise."

If this proverb is true, I should weigh 120 pounds, have a bank balance of six figures, and be able to explain to my kids what makes the wind blow.

I've always been an "early" person, whether it be for a doctor's appointment, sending out my Christmas cards, or going to bed. The adage, "Better late than never" has been banned from all cross-stitched samplers in our home.

I am lucky to stay awake for the nightly news. I can't tell you how many times I have kept myself awake for the opening theme song, only to be asleep before the anchor announces today's top story. And as for staying up until midnight to ring in the New Year, I go to bed at my usual time, content that somewhere, in some time zone, it is already tomorrow. Happy New Year to all, and to all a good night.

I get up at five in the morning. Every morning. Even weekends. Actually, I've tried to sleep late—or at least later (until six)—but my internal alarm clock insists on five. So I go with the flow.

Those early morning hours are precious to me. The house is quiet. There are no bowls of spilled cereal, broken shoelaces, or misplaced algebra assignments. One of the kitties may rub against my leg and meow a good morning but otherwise I have only the snap, crackle, pop of the house to keep me company.

Only that ... and God.

As I walk to my home office, cozy in sweatpants and sweatshirt, I snuggle into the Queen Anne chair and open my Bible. Totally rested, and open to suggestion, I let God in.

Good morning, Lord. What do you want me to do today?

I read and pray. And try to listen. The conversation is simple and productive. Where prayers later in the day may be hurried or harried as the obligations of daily life intrude, the prayers said before sunrise are as soothing and satisfying as an afternoon rest in a hammock. I start the day refreshed, body, mind, and soul. As I turn on my computer to begin writing about him, I am often reminded of a line from the Twila Paris song, "I Will Listen":

> "Can't imagine what the future holds,
> but I've already made my choice.
> And this is where I stand until he moves me on,
> and I will listen to his voice."*

I'm willing to tolerate the playful jabs made by the ignorant concerning my modest night life. What I accomplish in the morning before anyone is awake outshines any nocturnal diversions of the stay-up-late crowd who sleep until noon. They brag that they stay up late because it is exciting and gives them pleasure.

If they only knew what they were missing.

For there is nothing more exciting than feeling close to God. And nothing more pleasurable than taking a quiet stand and listening to his voice—in the stillness of the morning.

Role-Playing

*In the Lord, however, woman is not independent
of man, nor is man independent of woman.*
1 CORINTHIANS 11:11

A husband plays many roles. Mark is chief breadwinner, chief bread-eater, and designated driver on long vacations. He is assigned to make all batches of hard fudge, kill all wasps, and wash all vehicles. He is the one who plays catch with our aspiring athletes, pays the restaurant bill, and keeps me informed as to the stats on our favorite football team. It is his responsibility to remember our anniversary, to notice a new perm (he often fails at this one), and to keep my feet warm on the couch.

A wife plays many roles. I am the chief chicken-fryer, chocolate-eater, and designated packer for all vacations. I am assigned to make all lemon meringue pies, kill all dust bunnies, and wash all socks. I am the one who edits the reports of our aspiring writers, figures the taxes, and keeps Mark informed as to the stats of our extended families. It is my responsibility to remind him of our anniversary, to notice a new haircut (I often fail at this one), and to keep his feet warm on the couch.

These roles are the result of twenty-two years of compromise and fine tuning. When we first got married I had no clue as to what hard fudge *was*, much less the intricacies of making it as sugary as possible. And Mark had no clue as to the complexities of remembering the birthdays of our combined, ever-growing families. These were things we learned by necessity and through concession, the result being that our lives are now calmer and more organized. They actually contain extended moments of contentment. We've got the bugs worked out. Now we can enjoy.

Yet beyond the roles we assumed out of need, and the love, finely honed out of good intentions, the role I value the most is that of *friend*. Being in love is fine. Being partners in the day-to-day doings of our lives is great. But being best friends is awesome.

If you think being in love with your spouse requires a long-term commitment, consider being best friends. Friendship can be more sensual than love. It involves the entire body: the workings of the brain, the sentiment of the heart, the comfort of the arms, the strength of the shoulders, the readiness of the ears, the touch of the hands ... it lasts hours and weeks and years. Friendship is a sign of true commitment.

I'll play the other roles that have cropped up over the years. I'll be an overseer, a nutritionist, a consultant. I'll dust the furniture, dig the petunias, and drive the carpools—sometimes willingly and sometimes not. But the one role I take the greatest pride in is that of friend.

Mark and I are husband and wife. But more than that we are buddies—until death do us part.

part 4

He and Me

God is patient, kind, loving, and merciful.
I'm . . . not.

Taming the Firecracker

Let your gentleness be evident to all.

PHILIPPIANS 4:5

I wasn't always the warm, approachable paragon of niceness I am now. Although I still have my moments when I clench my teeth under my smile, it used to be worse. Before God renovated my heart, I was a tad impatient with the world. Case in point: when I used to do the bookkeeping for our sub-contracting business....

I would tap my pencil against the desk while the person at the other end of the line made small talk. The usual, "How's business?" "How 'bout those Cornhuskers?"....

I would feel my heart race like it was a lit fuse.

Enough already! I don't have time for this!

I would give short, clipped answers, knowing I was being rude but not caring. I would tuck the phone under my chin and take out the pile of checks I had to sign. At least I could do two things at—

"I'll call back when you're not busy," the voice on the phone would say. "Sorry to bother you."

Click. I would stare at the receiver. My gut wrenched—a feeling of guilt I handily shoved aside. Until the next time. And the time after that.

I was a ... not a nice person.

I had the usual excuses. I had three kids. My husband and I owned a commercial flooring company where I handled all the accounting in thirty hours a week. I was trying to write the

Great American Novel in my spare time and I was performing in *My Fair Lady* at the community playhouse which meant I had rehearsals every evening until ten. I was frazzled, frustrated, and frantic. And brutally frank.

Actually, a part of me enjoyed acting tough. It gave me power. I was a Supermom. A firecracker. Firecrackers are pleasing, aren't they?

As long as you don't get too close.

Turns out this firecracker was ready to pop—or fizzle out.

It started with my body. I began to experience some disturbing physical aftereffects following each of my rude phone encounters. Nothing dramatic, no chest-clutching warning signals to prove I'd become a type-A personality. More subtle. After hanging up the phone I would find myself shaking. My breath would come in short bursts. My heart would race and my voice would quiver. It took minutes to get myself under control. And the feeling of power found itself sharing space with shame. It was not a good combination.

But these physical symptoms were not enough to quench my fire. My daughter, Emily, did that with a single sentence.

It was a Saturday and we were busy with errands. I had a mental list of six places we needed to stop. If we hurried, we could get all the tasks accomplished and still be home in time to work on my weekend project—cleaning out the garage. We rushed into the parking lot of a retail store. I tossed my keys in my purse.

Emily hesitated getting out of the car.

"Come on," I said, grabbing a sack from the back seat. "I have to return this tape player. It's brand new but it doesn't rewind. I can't believe they make a tape player that breaks—"

"I'll wait in the car," Emily said, sliding down in her seat.

"Why don't you want to come in?"

"Because."

I shifted the sack under the other arm. "Emily ..."

She crossed her arms defensively. "Because you'll be rude. When things aren't right, you snap at people. It's embarrassing."

Rude? Me?

Rude. Me.

I leaned against the car door, digging into my memories. It was not a pleasant exercise. Rudeness had become second nature. It was a habit. A habit I needed to defuse.

I walked around the car to the passenger side. I opened Emily's door.

"You're absolutely right," I said, holding out my hand for her to take. "Why don't you come with me and make sure I do it right."

The store replaced the faulty tape player, exchanging my smile for one of their own. A please, a thank-you, and a come again. My heart felt lighter. There was no rapid breathing. No quaver to my voice. Calm. Satisfaction.

"See, Mom?" Emily said as we headed on our next errand. "It's not so hard to be nice."

She was right. But the firecracker in me was stubborn. It took effort to snuff out rudeness and haste and replace them with consideration and calm. And not all of the firecracker was bad. I was still a super mom. As long as I took the time to cultivate the sparkle instead of the roar.

Fear Not!

Fear of man will prove to be a snare,
but whoever trusts in the Lord is kept safe.

PROVERBS 29:25

I'm afraid of fear. It's an emotion I'd rather not visit. And it's an emotion I definitely don't want my kids to visit. And yet fear and childhood are deeply entangled, like gnarled trees whose barren branches grab at lightning flashes in the sky while the rumble of thunder makes the earth shake—

Enough! We have an amazing power to get ourselves worked up over nothing. As a teenager I often watched the Saturday night *Creature Feature* (hosted by Dr. Sanguinary) alone in the basement. I'd wrap myself in a blanket and snuggle into the deep recesses of the Naugahyde chair so only my eyes would show. The lights were off (mood lighting for monsters) and the flickering of the movie cast strange shadows behind the sewing machine and the Ping Pong table. No matter how scared I got, it never occurred to me to shut off the TV. Maybe it was because I knew all monsters (at least in movies shown in the '60s) got their what-for in the end. Mankind prevailed and was victorious.

In the movie's aftermath, there was the problem of getting from the basement to my bedroom upstairs without the TV monsters grabbing me by the tail. As the credits rolled and I ventured from my cocoon to turn *on* the light and *off* the TV— in that order—I kept the blanket wrapped around me. Everyone knows that monsters cannot penetrate Orlon and wool (cotton is questionable). Without the noise of the TV, the silence of the house was deafening. But if I listened carefully, I could hear *them*, I could hear the monsters in the furnace room slithering around my dad's tools, their claws scratching on the floor as they made their way to the rec room to get—

I ran up the stairs. I tripped on the blanket. I could *feel* the monsters nipping at my heels and my spine tingled with their presence. I stumbled into the bedroom hallway only to stop dead in my tracks as I spotted a dark form—

"What's going on?" my mother asked, flipping on the hall light.

I gathered as much dignity as I could muster with flushed cheeks, wild eyes, and a blanket tangled around my legs. "Uh, uh ..."

"You scared yourself watching those monster movies again, didn't you?"

To prove her wrong I let the blanket pool at my feet, risking the cold rush of monster vibrations on my shoulders. I straightened my spineless spine and strode into my room. "I'm going to bed now," I proclaimed.

My mother smiled a knowing smile. "Do you want me to check your closet for bogeymen?" she asked.

"That won't be necessary." *I'll check the closet myself.*

I knew there were no bogeymen, no Frankensteins, no wolfmen, no gelatinous blobs from outer space. Yet once in awhile, I invited them into my life. Why? Was it so I could conquer them? Was I that desperate for a thrill or a victory?

As I grew older I discovered there were plenty of real things to be afraid of. Such as going away to college, getting married—or not getting married. Bills, kids, failure, wrinkles ...

I didn't need to invite fear into my life. It was all around me. Sometimes I'd find myself worried about being worried. What if the worst happened? What would I do if ... I gave fear a lot of power it didn't deserve.

My niece Brittney started kindergarten this year. As Halloween approached, the school counselor talked to the kids about fear, mentioning that she used to have a ritual before bedtime where she would check under her bed and in her closet for any monsters. Brittney raised her hand and said, "My Dad won't allow monsters in *our* house."

It's so simple. We'll never have to worry about being afraid, about checking our lives for the bogeymen and monsters—if we don't allow them into our house. And how do we do that?

By snatching the power away from fear and giving it to God. Now that's a thrill. That's a victory.

A Gray Thumb

I made it beautiful with abundant branches,
the envy of all the trees of Eden
in the garden of God.

EZEKIEL 31:9

B irds sing, bees buzz, warm breezes blow. And my thumb
starts to twitch.

Ah, she's a gardener, you say. *Her green thumb aches with the
ancient instinct to be one with the earth; to make things grow.*

Wrong.

My green thumb wilted long ago, leaving me with an appendage that tends toward gray.

The fact that marigolds and impatiens wither under my gaze does not prevent me from trying. Each spring, in spite of my bleak history, I feel a compulsion to be part of God's renewal process. I sit on the front porch and measure the progress of the budding trees that are lucky enough to thrive without my intervention. I tour the yard with Mark and marvel how the lawn greens up and the bushes spring to life without human meddling (at least *my* human meddling).

I want to help but I know my limitations. Not everyone can be good at gardening. Some people are good cooks, some are great athletes, some thrill to an organized, dust-free house....

Never mind.

Unfortunately, Mark is a die-hard optimist. Every year he drags me to the garden store where he hopes to conquer my fears by meeting them head-on....

A teenager, looking ridiculously tanned, directs traffic, guiding us to a parking place in the back forty. *Certainly a tram will pick us up like it does at the amusement park?* I tell Mark I'll wait in the car. He pries me out with the Jaws of Life.

I enter the store. The swarm of people envelops me—alien people; people who drool over sacks of manure and think grass stains on their knees are *de rigueur*. The potted plants look up with hopeful petals: *Buy me! Buy me!*

Mark pulls me to a flat of begonias and notes that these are the flowers which thrive in the entry to our neighborhood every year.

"No one gives them constant care and they survive," he says.

Sure, make me feel guilty. I remind him I tried begonias last year. The leaves folded under and the blossoms dropped so it looked as if we'd been visited by a wayward flower girl sprinkling her carpet of petals.

"How about roses?" he asks. "You love roses."

He's half right. I love to *receive* roses—delivered from a florist. He has conveniently forgotten my attempt at rose gardening; how the stems grew to a gangling mass that Prince Charming couldn't have hacked his way through. And not a rose to be had.

"I'll just hike back to the car—"

"Wait!" he says, knowing he's losing me. "How about geraniums? They can't be hard to grow. Everybody has geraniums."

Although I realize I'm setting myself up for failure when my geraniums are the only ones in the entire free world to wilt, I nod. It's a matter of self-preservation. If I don't leave soon, I will be drawn into the Cult of the Green Thumb and will find myself buying gardening gloves with little bows at the wrists and a matching sit-upon.

We escape into the afternoon with ten sacks of decorative bark, six geraniums, and a new hand spade since I accidentally-on-purpose lost the one from last year. When we get home I mention that the Christmas decorations should be organized. I feel an absurd need to start on next year's taxes.

Mark doesn't buy it, even when I put a hand to my forehead and exclaim I feel feverish. He whacks my palm with the new hand spade like a surgeon's assistant handing over a scalpel. I shuffle off to tempt fate.

A half-hour later, the geraniums are planted. I retire for the day.

For the first week, I am Nature's little helper. I water my geraniums; I even sit nearby encouraging them to grow. I pray that God will ignore my limitations and do his stuff. But by the second week, it happens. They realize they are not in the hands of a pro. They are not getting breakfast in bed every morning like they did at the nursery, and they are not having those annoying weeds plucked so their roots can freely unfold. I see a flicker of panic in their petals as the blush of hope fades. Then their chlorophyll runs cold. They shrivel and die.

I pull their withered roots from the cold, cold ground wondering what lesson I'm supposed to learn from the experience (persistence or humility?). I push the decorative bark over the bare holes. Mark pretends not to notice. We never speak of it again.

Until next year. *Asters might be pretty ...*

A Straight Head

*Hide your face from my sins
and blot out all my iniquity.
Create in me a pure heart, O God,
and renew a steadfast spirit within me.*

PSALM 51:9-10

I was in a bad mood.

I was snappish as a pair of pantyhose. It was one of those days when I knew I shouldn't bark at the kids—but I did anyway. I knew I should fold the laundry before wrinkles took up permanent residence—but I let it sit. It was a day when Ebenezer Scrooge looked like the perfect role model. Bah humbug.

Pity the poor salespeople who called, wanting to clean my carpets, take my picture, and insure my worldly goods. Growl, hiss, slam.

Pity my poor kitchen floor which suffered the spilled flour, smashed egg, and dribbled milk of my slapdash mood.

Pity my poor children who scurried to the furthest corners of the house as they wisely revised the old maxim to "Children should *not* be seen *or* heard." Truth be told, I wanted to hide away just like them, to be left alone to wallow in my mood.

And it wasn't even noon....

"Mom?"

I whipped around to see Laurel. "What?" I snapped.

She held up one of her dolls—which was minus a head.

"Can you fix it?" she asked.

I took the two parts of the doll and studied the problem.

"She's had a bad day," said Laurel. "Just like you."

"There's no *had* about it," I said, "I'm *having* a bad day."

"Can you fix it?"

Fix it? How could I fix such a totally ruined day?

The doll's head popped onto her neck. I made a final adjustment, aligning her nose and her toes. I handed the doll to Laurel and she skipped away, content I had fixed everything.

But I hadn't.

I stepped outside onto the deck and leaned against the railing. It was a beautiful day. Why hadn't I noticed? There was no excuse.

I took a deep breath and let the cool breeze drive away the negative thoughts that controlled my mind. I closed my eyes and let the sunshine relax my brittle face. I let the sounds of the birds weave their way into my vacant heart. I let the smell of freshly cut grass and spring flowers remind me that all things can be renewed.

I could be renewed.

I'm ashamed, Lord. I'm ashamed and sorry for wasting so much of the day you've given me. Help me to start over and do it right.

I went inside and called the kids. It was time for them to come out—now that their mother had her head on straight.

Just Because

Delight yourself in the Lord
and he will give you the desires of your heart.

PSALM 37:4

I'm a ham. Give me a show tune, point me toward an audi-ence, and it will be next Tuesday before I stop singing.

All this exuberance doesn't mean I'm a great singer. I'm good, but miles from great. What I lack in talent (I'm as far from Barbra Streisand and Sandi Patti as hamburger is from filet mignon) I make up in willingness to do whatever it takes. The show must go on!

When I found out our community chorus was going to sing a medley from *The Phantom of the Opera*, I felt the first stirring of desire. To sing one of Christine's songs—preferably in Victorian garb—would fulfill my lifelong need to perform and wear pretty costumes (the fancier the better).

The tryouts were at six-thirty and I was running late due to the fact I rarely fill my car with gas before it's begging for it. I had to choose between filling up or walking home. It only fol-lowed that there were no parking places within shouting dis-tance of the building where the tryouts were being held. After cruising up and down the aisles in vain, I zoomed into a parking space in the boonies and ran to the chorus room: six thirty-five.

"Nancy, are you ready to go?" the director asked.

As soon as my pulse stops pounding at one-forty and I can take a breath deeper than a gasp.

I followed him into the rehearsal room, trying to calm my

breathing. In, out. Slower. In. Out. He played the introduction. I sang, grabbing a breath every other note. *He must think I have the lung capacity of a flea.*

"May I start over?" I asked. The butterflies in my stomach which usually did double loops during any tryout were now divebombing my toes.

Kind man that he was, he gave me another chance.

Please, God. Help me to do my best.

One more deep breath. I sang the song. It was better—not great—but definitely better.

I left the tryout resigned to failure—especially when I heard the next woman sing. That's it. She's got it. I'm a goner.

I said another prayer. *Whatever you want, Lord. I'll leave it up to you.*

∽

The next week, when I came to the chorus room, I braced myself. Whoever had been chosen would be listed on the board.

My name was on the board.

I got it!

Thank you, thank you, thank you. I felt humbled and undeserving. Obviously, the director (and the Lord) had listened beyond the voice I showed them during the tryout. And somehow, that made the victory even sweeter. Why was God being so nice to me? What had I done for him lately?

I worked hard on the part—in the shower, making dinner, driving to the dentist. My family learned the song well enough to sing along (perhaps we could do a quintet?). As the concert neared, I asked the director if he wanted to use costumes. I just happened to have in my possession a gorgeous dress I usually wore for the Dickens festival ... I was disappointed when he said no. He didn't want to bother with it. I resigned myself to his decision, thankful that I got to sing the part I wanted—even without the fantasy of wearing a glorious costume.

But God wasn't done handing out special gifts.

It was the night of the last rehearsal. We were practicing on stage and the director told me and the man who was singing Raoul's part to stay afterward for a few minutes. He had an idea. I assumed he had some blocking changes. I did not expect him to say, "I've been thinking ... you said you had a costume you could wear?"

I sang the part of Christine wearing a teal and persimmon satin dress with satin roses crowning the shoulders. Sequins and beads sparkled on the black lace bodice. I felt like a princess. I sang like ... me.

On the way home from the concert, I thanked God over and over for making me so happy. I knew I didn't deserve it. I hadn't even asked for it. And yet he'd known my heart's desire and had given it to me.

Just because he loves me. Our God is an awesome God.

Me, Myself, and ...

Give, and it will be given to you. A good measure, pressed down, shaken together and running over, will be poured into your lap. For with the measure you use, it will be measured to you.

LUKE 6:38

I cruised the lot looking for the best parking place—the place closest to the grocery store.

I spotted the glow of brake lights in a parking space two stalls from the front door. Someone was backing out. I zoomed up the aisle, switching on my turn signal to claim it.

This one was mine, all mine. Pure satisfaction.

As I locked up the car and headed toward the store, I noticed another car searching for a parking place. An older woman, whose chin barely cleared the top of the steering wheel, peered hopefully down the rows of cars. I knew she'd end up parking at the far end of the parking lot. I'd been lucky. I'd been at the right place at the right time to get the best spot in the lot.

Before I went inside the store, I gave one last glance at the hapless woman in her quest for a decent parking space. My feeling of satisfaction gave way to shame.

There was no reason I needed to grab a spot so close to the store. I wasn't juggling a stroller, a diaper bag, and a purse like some shoppers. I was healthy and agile. And yet I had claimed the best parking space with as much greed as if it had been a treasure chest heaped with gold.

I'd taken what I didn't need, just to have it.

Fifteen minutes later, while deciding whether a twenty-eight-ounce can of fruit cocktail for $1.39 was a better buy than an eighteen-ounce can for eighty-nine cents, I happened to spot the older woman I'd seen in the parking lot. A wooden cane hung from the side of her shopping cart. She gripped the handle of the cart as if it were her lifeline. The wheel of her cart squeaked and wobbled precariously.

Heel. Cad. Selfish polecat.

As we passed in the aisle I flashed her a guilty smile, making silent amends. She returned the smile warily, her eyes asking the question, "Do I know you?"

I continued shopping for my family of five, stopping only when the eight-pack of toilet paper refused to balance on top of the leaning tower of frozen pizza. I headed for the checkout lane. Three checkers were on duty. I scanned my options. A mother with a baby, loaded down with disposable diapers, jars of baby food, and a bottle of Tylenol; a man stocking up for a month of Sundays; and a woman in a business suit buying a birthday cake and a card.

Another cart snuck into my line of sight. A contender for the shortest line. Her cart rivaled mine, a box of Cheerios sliding into a loaf of bread. It was either her or me.

I zipped in line behind the birthday girl. Cheerios-and-bread had to settle for the line behind the mother with the now-crying baby.

Boy, was I smart.

I was just settling into smugness, when I heard the squeak of a wheel. I looked up. It was her.

The old woman followed the route I had taken moments before, eyeing the checkout lanes to see which one would keep her on her feet for the shortest amount of time. She pulled into the lane beside me.

I looked at her cart—you could actually see the bottom of it. I looked at mine. Ten layers separated the toilet paper from the crushed eggs. I glanced forward to the birthday girl who was now getting her change.

Acting on impulse, I said to the older woman, "Why don't you go in front of me?" I pulled my cart back to make room for her. I caught the toilet paper before it dumped itself onto the floor.

"Thank you, dear. How kind of you to think of me."

Think of her? She didn't know about the parking lot, how I'd snatched the closest place. She didn't know how I'd won the race for the shortest checkout lane, edging out Cheerios-and-bread by using my finely-honed skill to grab the best for myself.

Guilt made me avoid her eyes. I busied myself flipping through the magazines. "100 Ways to Cook Salami." "How to Lose 50 Pounds Off Your Hips." *"How to Be a More Giving Person"* ...

The bagger asked, "Paper or plastic?" The woman paid. But before she left she turned to me one more time.

"Thanks again for thinking of me," she said.

I blushed, her gratitude drowning my guilt. "Anytime," I said. I watched the bagger carry the woman's groceries outside, her hand balanced on his arm.

The checker took the pesky toilet paper from my cart, ran it across the scanner, and asked, "How are you today?"

"Fine," I said. But I didn't feel fine.

As the checker delved into the second layer of groceries I said a silent prayer. "Lord, forgive me. You give me so much and yet

I'm never satisfied. Help me to give more than I take."

Pulling out of the parking lot, I tested my new resolve by letting another car in front of me. The driver waved his thanks. This wasn't so bad. Not bad at all. I felt an inner glow as God answered my prayer. *Stop grabbing the best* for yourself *and start giving the best* of yourself.

I knew replacing my selfish power with God's power wouldn't be easy. It would take work. But I also knew he would help me—one parking place at a time.

Let's Make a Deal

Who has known the mind of the Lord?
Or who has been his counselor?
Who has ever given to God,
that God should repay him?

ROMANS 11:34-35

The trading at the New York Stock Exchange is nothing compared to the trading that goes on in our house.

"If you set the table for me today, I'll do it for you tomorrow," Emily says to Carson.

"If you'll play school with me," Laurel says, "I'll play Battleship with you."

"If you get your homework done, you can watch TV," I say.

Then there's always the wise guy: "I'll clean my room, if Mom gives up sweets."

No way.

At last count, our family has traded enough shares in the moments of our lives to keep the economy of the United States buzzing into the next century. There's nothing wrong with making a few deals. It's a way to make things even, like splitting a Hershey bar in two and holding out the pieces for the other person to chose. Everybody wins.

But something goes astray when I try to make a deal with God.

When we moved to the Kansas City area from Lincoln, Nebraska, we purchased a wonderful home with plentiful closets and a hundred-year-old oak tree gracing the front lawn.

Unfortunately, we hadn't sold our equally nice house back in Lincoln. Double house payments, double insurance, double utilities. A homeowner's nightmare.

We didn't worry about it much. Too busy unpacking boxes. Hanging curtains. Finding the perfect place for the antique pitcher with the chipped spout. The first double house payment came and went with only a slight cringe. Surely the house would sell soon. Things like that always worked out for us.

Not this time.

Three months. Six. Nine.

The presence of the Lincoln house suffocated our peace of mind like a wool blanket on an August afternoon. We dropped the price. We ripped out the carefully selected wallpaper and painted the walls white, neutralizing our once cozy home into a home for Any Man.

And we prayed. A lot.

Nothing happened.

I began to question whether I was praying correctly. Was there a secret word or phrase that would unlock the answer to our prayers?

Or maybe God was open to a deal....

If he would find a buyer for the house I would take care of our new home until it glowed like a lantern in the Kansas night. I would wax, polish, shine … but I knew myself too well. *I'll clean the garage tomorrow. There's a movie on TV I've been wanting to see …*

Another deal. "If you'll sell the house, Lord, I'll never bark at the kids again. I'll be patient and kind. I'll speak softly: *OK, who left the milk on the counter?*"

And another. "We'll go to church every Sunday. No excuses."

But the trees were so beautiful. The golds, reds, and russets simply begged us to go for a drive Sunday morning and then we stopped and had a picnic....

Ten months. Eleven. Thousands of dollars. Savings plundered.

Apparently, dealing with God wasn't as simple as doing extra chores in exchange for a trip to the ice cream store. It didn't help that my bargains were shallow and short-lived. I came to believe there was nothing I could do to make him act. Nothing I could give God that would equal his share of the candy bar.

That wasn't true. There was one thing I could give him that was worth something—as long as I gave it with no strings attached.

Trust.

It was the hardest thing I ever did, giving our Nebraska home to God. *Take it, it's yours. Do with it whatever you want—*

The house sold.

I have no idea why God made us wait so long. Perhaps if I were a faster learner ... but no. I'm trying to fathom the unfathomable.

The fact is, God gives us what we need when he decides we need it. Period.

No deals.

Hey, Over Here!

Where can I go from your Spirit?
Where can I flee from your presence?

PSALM 139:7

"**M**ommy, we're stuck!" Three-year-old Carson sat in the backseat of the car and told me what I already knew. Our car was stuck in eight inches of mud.

On that particular March day I won the booby prize for patience (or my lack thereof). The road near our neighborhood was being widened. During construction the road was closed and detoured—a three mile detour.

As I liked detours almost as much as I liked sitting in the waiting room at the doctor's office, I decided to consider the "Road Closed" sign a mere suggestion. Tossing common sense aside, I took a shortcut around the sign. All I had to do was drive thirty feet on dirt and I could hook up with the main road. No problem.

Problem.

There was no dirt. Only mud. Lots of slimy, oozing, greedy mud that surrounded the tires of my car and held it captive.

The mud pulled at my boots with powerful suction as I walked around the car assessing the degree of my stupidity. First-degree, definitely first-degree. The tires were deep in muddy ruts, the saturated ground enclosing them on all sides like quicksand in an old Tarzan movie. All I needed was a pith helmet and I would fit right in.

As I got back in the car, I decided to do what any mature,

responsible mother would do. I cried. And Carson, not wanting to be left out, joined in. At least our cries were compatible— mine in the key of G and his in a higher C.

"Don't cry," I told him. With the deep resilience of a toddler he stopped his wailing as if I'd pulled the plug. He handed me his half-eaten, slightly soggy graham cracker. "No thanks, sweetie. It's all yours."

I pulled out a tissue and dried my tears and his messy hands.

"We need a bit of divine intervention here, don't we?" I said. Carson nodded and crammed the rest of the cracker in his mouth.

Practicality took over and a plan of sorts formed in my mind. *I'll have to call a tow truck.* Carson and I would walk the mile or so to the closest house—which happened to belong to a friend of mine. I grabbed my keys and Carson. I locked the doors, took a step away from the car, and froze. What had I just done—locked the doors so no one would steal my car? I laughed. If a thief could steal it, he could *have* it.

Carrying Carson on one hip, I slogged through the quagmire, heading toward the pavement. The heavy mud added two sizes to my already ample feet and a zillion pounds to my ample figure. Each step was an effort. It didn't take me long to realize that my plan needed revision. Carson—who weighed in at a chubby thirty-five pounds—was too heavy for me to carry the mile to my friend's house, and the one mile to my friend's house was too far for Carson to walk. I glanced down the street and saw that it was empty of any potentially helpful cars.

After all, who would drive down this way when the road is closed?

As I neared the pavement, intent on maneuvering around the Road Closed sign without dumping Carson in the mud, I didn't hear the car's engine. But when I looked up, there it was—coming toward us.

"Where did that car come from?" I asked the air. "No one was around a moment ago."

The woman driving the car stopped and opened the passenger door. She was a nice-looking brunette in her late thirties. A Garfield key chain dangled from the ignition. I remembered all my childhood lessons about taking a ride with a stranger. But anyone who liked Garfield couldn't be half bad. Besides, at this moment she looked like an angel.

"Would you like a ride?" she asked me.

She didn't need to ask twice. I put Carson in the back seat and opened the passenger door. "Could you take us to my friend's house just up the road?"

"You bet." The woman turned around and drove slowly as I kept my muddy feet hanging out the door of the car. As I rambled on about getting stuck and my own foolishness for doing so, the woman said, "You know, it's funny. I've never been down this street before. In fact, I was late for an appointment and came down this street on an impulse to try and make up some time. It's lucky I did."

I looked at her and smiled. I thought of divine intervention. Luck had nothing to do with it.

Make Your Selection, Please

Come and see what God has done,
how awesome his works in man's behalf!

PSALM 66:5

When I'm trying to sort through a problem, I do two things: I pray and I eat chocolate. One feeds my soul and the other, my sweet tooth.

On one particularly busy day, I was bothered by a particularly pesky problem. So as I buzzed through my to-do list, I prayed—at the stoplight, while waiting for the dry cleaning, while going through the carwash. I didn't pray in generalities, but prayed *very* specifically. I wanted God to get it right. Hopefully, he would agree with my solution, give his blessings, and everything would be grand.

As talking to heaven made me want to taste a bit of it, I eventually took a chocolate break.

The coins clattered down the vending machine's innards. Chocolate delicacies called to me like sirens wooing Odysseus. Did I want rich and gooey (Snickers), rich and creamy (Reese's peanut butter cups), or rich and crunchy (Butterfingers)? If only I had enough calorie reserves to have them all.

And the winner was: rich and gooey. I pulled the knob under the Snickers bar.

Nothing happened.

I yanked the knob again. Harder. Maybe it didn't understand the laws of elementary vending?

The Snickers sat there, leering at me. Gloating.

After a quick glance around the vending area for witnesses, I gave the machine a smack with my fist. The Snickers held firm. But its neighbor, a low-fat granola bar, plunged into the tray.

"No!"

I retrieved the granola bar and stared at it. *How dare it presume to take the place of decadent chocolate!*

I dug out more money. I fed the machine a second time and carefully pulled the Snickers knob.

Nothing.

I grabbed the sides of the vending machine and leaned against it. "You're not listening!"

I pulled the knob again, pounding the glass above the Snickers at the same time, hoping to give it a push.

A granola bar plunged off the edge to its death.

"No! No!"

I put a hand to my forehead, took a deep breath, and tried to calm myself. My desire for the Snickers bar was nearing the obsession level. I didn't *want* it anymore, I *needed* it.

I rummaged around the bottom of my purse hoping for a scattering of stray coins. If only the machine took pennies.

"Thirty-five. Forty." Just one more dime. I looked in the compartment that held my sunglasses. A crumpled receipt, a peppermint, a lint ball … and a dime!

I stroked the front of the machine, calming it. "I'm going to try this one more time," I said. "For your own good, and my sanity, please cooperate."

I inserted the coins with delicate precision, giving the machine ample time to log in each new addition. I had the Snickers knob in my hand when I hesitated. *I've pulled the*

Snickers knob twice and gotten a granola bar twice. Therefore, it's only logical ...

I moved my hand to the granola bar's knob. I bothered God with a chocolate prayer and pulled.

A low-fat granola bar fell into the tray.

I closed my eyes and stifled a scream. With cool deliberation I stuck the three granola bars into my purse, turned my back on the vending machine, and strode to the parking lot. With amazing self-control, I held in my anger until I was alone in my car.

I hit the steering wheel with the palm of my hand. "Stupid machine!" I said. "I gave it the right amount of change, I made the selection, I pulled the knob. I did everything right and yet it didn't listen to me! It kept giving me what I didn't want."

I yanked a granola bar from my purse and ripped off the wrapper. I tore a bite off the top and chewed vigorously as if exacting my revenge.

My chewing slowed. *Not bad. Not bad at all.* I took another bite and read the back of the wrapper. It was certainly more nutritious than a candy bar. Less fat, even a few vitamins.

"Well, what do you know?" I said aloud. "I pay the machine, pound the machine, stroke the machine, try to outwit the machine. I ask over and over for one particular thing and it doesn't listen. Then it turns out, the thing it's giving me is better than what I asked for."

Unannounced, my pesky problem popped into my thoughts. I called up the prayer I'd been reciting and reeled it off. I stopped in mid-sentence and stared at the granola bar.

Had I been treating God like a vending machine: prayer in, answer out? Had I been *paying* him with prayers, *pounding* him with my persistence, *stroking* him with easy platitudes, trying to *outwit* him by asking over and over for his blessings on *my* will? Was he offering me something that would be better for me than what I asked for?

I put the granola bar aside and bowed my head. "I'm sorry for my selfish nagging, Lord. Thank you for the lesson. You know my problem and you know the right answer. Show me what *you* have in mind. I know it will be the best solution for everyone."

As I pulled onto the street, I knew my problem would be solved. Wisely, fairly, mercifully ... and if I was really blessed, sweetened with the heavenly taste of chocolate.

Getting the Timing Right

*Perseverance must finish its work so that you may
be mature and complete, not lacking anything.*

JAMES 1:4

My continuous desire for chocolate delicacies spurred me
to cook and taught me that timing is everything.

Sort of. It should be noted that I am a great heater-upper
and a marginal stirrer, qualities that have kept my family from
starving and the local restaurants thriving. As far as timing goes,
I happen to believe that "now" (or sooner) should be the
answer to all my requests made both to humans—and God.

How my culinary skills were improved, and my realization
that God has the timing business under control, came about
because of a newspaper article.

Reading the food section of the newspaper one day (only
because someone had run off with the front page), I noticed an
article about Maida Heatter, a woman who'd made a name for
herself in the dessert world. Her cookbooks were supposedly
foolproof. Since my many flub-ups in the kitchen had christened me a fool, I figured we were perfect for each other.

So I purchased one of Maida's cookbooks and presented
myself to Mark. "I'm going to become good at making *one*
thing in the kitchen," I announced.

"Making a mess?" he said.

Cynic.

"No," I said. "I'm going to become a chocolate gourmet."

"You already are," he said. "We should buy stock in
Hershey's."

"You're not listening," I said, brandishing the cookbook proudly. "I'm going to cook chocolate delicacies."

"As in mix together?"

"Yes."

"And put in the oven?"

"Yes."

"And eat?"

Oh, ye of little faith.

I showed him my back and strode to a chair to read my cookbook (in itself an alien idea, as most of my recipes came from the backs of boxes).

Two springform pans, a pastry bag, double boiler, and other sundry nonessential essentials later, he saw how serious I was. Having put Maida's book behind a clear plastic cookbook holder (I'm a connoisseur of splatters) I vowed to do something I'd never tried before: follow directions.

I reintroduced myself to my measuring cups and dug the one-half teaspoon out from behind the corn-on-the-cob holders.

In a bowl that's free of grease (an oxymoron in my kitchen) *separate eggs, being careful not to get any egg yolk in the whites. In a small glass bowl, whip egg whites until they hold a firm shape but are not stiff or dry. Do not over-beat.*

Too many variables. Grease, yolks, size, glass, time. And what about the warning? How firm is firm? How can an egg white be dry? I'm a visual person. I needed specific examples. *Beat until the egg whites are stiffer than the face cream you slather on your skin and less stiff than the snowdrift you plowed into last January.*

Laurel entered my new domain. She carried the mail.

"Mom, you got a rejection in the mail—"

"Not now!" I yelled. "I'm watching egg whites."

"Watching them do what?" she asked.

"Whip themselves into a frenzy," I said.

She moved a safe distance away to watch me watch.

"Who's the rejection from?" I asked, my eyes glued to the frothing white mixture.

She informed me which particular publisher was *not* interested in seeing my book manuscript—a decision I hoped they would forever regret.

"I get so tired of waiting," I whined. "When is it going to be *my* time?"

Laurel set the mail aside and pointed to the bowl of white peaks. "It's *their* time, Mom," she said.

"Maybe," I said. "But I'm not sure. The timing is so tricky."

"How long?" she asked.

"I don't know," I said, frantically rereading the cookbook, hoping for some blatant clues. "The right amount of time. Not too soon and not too—"

"Mom!"

Laurel pointed to the bowl. The egg whites had deflated as if a plug had been pulled.

"What happened?" she asked.

I stared at the spinning bowl. I turned off the mixer, defeated.

"It's not fair," I said. "Who made these timing rules anyway?"

"Wow," Laurel said, coming closer to peer into the bowl. "One moment it's right and the next it's wrong. Why, Mom?"

"Who knows?"

"But why?" she asked.

Was there a life-lesson amid the egg whites? *Because that's the way it is, that's the way God wants it.* One moment it's right and the next it's wrong.

I dumped the eggs into the sink and cleaned out the bowl.

"Are you starting over?" Laurel asked.

As I headed to the refrigerator for more eggs I glanced at the rejection sitting on the counter.

"You bet I am," I said. "I'll keep trying until the timing's right."

Because timing is everything. Not my timing. God's timing.

No Sweat

I pray that you may enjoy good health and that all may go well with you, even as your soul is getting along well.

3 JOHN 1:2

Our bodies are a temple. We should treat them with respect; keep them healthy. Eat foods that aren't dripping in fat. And most importantly, ex ... exer ...

I find it hard to say—and even harder to do. *Exercise.*

I'd walk. I'd do sit-ups with the best of them. If it weren't for one thing.

Sweat.

I know a surefire way to make a million bucks. Find a way to exercise and not sweat.

No matter what you call it—sweat, perspiration, or that salty glow you get when your lungs are burning—it's annoying. It stings your eyes, melts your makeup, and leaves telltale half-moons under your arms. It's the pits—literally.

I realize a sweaty brow is a trophy of sorts. It is proof (if accompanied by the appropriate ball, racquet, or jogging attire) that you are keeping the inner workings of your temple healthy by achieving a measure of fitness. Exactly what measure can be determined by your posture. If you are in a prone position resembling a dead gingerbread man, your fitness quotient is low. If you are jogging in place with enough breath left in your lungs to recite the Declaration of Independence, I don't want to speak to you.

Some weekend warriors (like me) don't need a Boston Marathon to break into a respectable sweat. Folding fitted sheets, sitting through my son's band concert for an hour and a half, or turning the channels manually on the TV when the remote gives out, can all create a respectable glow. When I attempt some real exercise like walking, tennis, or a game of H-O-R-S-E, my body calls out the National Guard. This is not a drill.

There have been obvious improvements in the sweat department in the past hundred years. Before the advent of deodorant, daily showers, and washers that use electricity instead of the nearest rock, the aroma of mankind was an accepted part of everyday life. But considering that lice, outdoor privies, and dirt floors were also customary in those days, it wasn't a point to brag about. The pomander many of us have sitting in a pretty dish to freshen a room used to be a part of standard attire, hanging from one's belt to mask the aroma of one's toils. People died young, not from disease, but because their noses gave out.

Now we live in a perfumed society. There is no excuse for not smelling like roses, a newborn baby, musk, or a sea breeze. But there's still that other problem: the moisture problem. I know antiperspirants are supposed to reduce or prevent perspiration. Yeah, right. When you've just mowed the lawn or washed the car in time for it to rain, your antiperspirant surrenders and ... you sweat.

Sweat discriminates. Andre Agassi and Kristi Yamaguchi look great in sweat. I, however, look wilted—my face gets red, my hair hangs like cold spaghetti, and my clothes stick to me in all the wrong places. Perhaps it has something to do with our respective earning capacities.

I realize sweat has a purpose (as do rice cakes and Richard Simmons—or so they say), but certainly someone can design a pill that will cool our bodies without making them sticky and uncomfortable. Dogs pant. Humans … ? If they could combine this new cooling pill with a way to make Cheetos and malted milk balls good for you, they've got their first investor.

So, take note, all you closet inventors. Find a way to make our temples perspiration-free and the world will kiss your sweet-smelling feet.

No sweat.

Don't Hurry Worry

*Do not be anxious about anything, but in every-
thing, by prayer and petition, with thanksgiving, present your requests to God.*

PHILIPPIANS 4:6

If I got a penny for every time I worried, I'd be sitting in a
Swiss chalet watching other people ski. I'm a professional
worrier—have been since a penny bought something.

God will take care of everything.

I *know* that. But giving up worry is as easy as giving up my
pink fuzzy slippers, my movie copy of *Gone with the Wind,* my
very old but much-loved pillow.

It's not that I don't trust God. But I figure he has to be
swamped, what with Bosnia, Africa, the Middle East ...
Certainly he doesn't need to be bothered by a bevy of everyday
concerns rising up from Kansas. Worries about Carson's math,
Emily's history, and Laurel's spelling tests; my husband's fatigue
from dealing with seven hundred phone calls at work before
noon; my impatience because I'm not a best-selling author yet.

So what if I handle a few things on my own? Is that so bad?

Yup.

But I'm an independent woman! I can install a light switch
without shocking myself; I can mow the lawn with only one
five-minute nap behind the azalea bush; and I can whip up
homemade treats for Girl Scouts with ten minutes' notice (take
Chips Ahoy cookies out of package and place in Tupperware
container). Surely God likes independent people.

Nope.

I discovered this truth when the ravioli boiled over.

It was the end of a soap-opera day. Not the typical soap opera where my long lost sister, a nympho-schizo who ran away with my fourth husband once removed, appears on my doorstep, while my evil neighbor plots to torch my house because my clothes are whiter than hers (surely, you jest). *That* I could have handled.

It was a day when the cat piddled in the philodendron. We were out of milk ... and bread ... and eggs, forcing us to eat Doritos and orange juice for breakfast. Somehow, the kids managed to find a matching pair of shoes and most of their homework. One off to school. Two. Three.

I had just scooped up the kitty with all intentions of having a serious discussion detailing the differences between potting soil and kitty litter when Laurel called from school. She'd forgotten her library book—which was already two days overdue. She couldn't check out *Little House on the Prairie* until she returned *Little House in the Big Woods*. And her book report was due in three days. Grabbing the book and my car keys, I wondered if any twentieth-century family was as organized as Pa and Ma Ingalls. The modern world could be so ... trying.

After returning the book, I stopped at the school door. The sky had turned from blue to blanched—accompanied by a torrent of wet stuff. Never fear, my umbrella was ... in the car. I made a run for it, stifling the urge to rotate slowly in the rain, saving my clothes a trip through the washer at some later date.

While I was in a library sort of mood, I headed for the main branch. I needed to research the effects of oleander for the mystery I was writing. As the weather progressed from raining cats and dogs to dumping an entire pet store on my car, the windshield wipers chose to deviate from their normal 4/4 rhythm. They tried a quick waltz ... before giving up out of rhythmic frustration.

Brake lights! Oh, no! Whew ... a near miss. I collected my scattered wits and pulled into a gas station to replace the wiper blades. Unfortunately, they cost more than the seventy-three cents I dug out of the glove compartment. My checkbook was at home. Charge it.

The library, groceries, lunch, laundry, writing.

Finally, a hot bath. I was just sinking into the steaming water, having discovered a way to get my knees and torso warm at the same time, when the phone rang.

It was a neighbor who lived near Carson's school. He'd called to tell me Carson had fallen off his bike. His arm was broken.

I wrung out my hair, pulled on some clothes, and raced out the door. I found Carson sitting on the curb, his right arm held gently with his left hand. A few brave tears escaped. His, and mine.

Off to the hospital where he got X-rayed, delayed, and OK'd—and became the proud owner of a fluorescent green cast.

I zoomed home, planted Carson on the couch armed with the remote control. I considered making him chicken soup (feed a cold, starve ... an arm?). I wondered how he would do homework with his right hand encased in its glow-in-the-dark prison.

I headed for the kitchen to start dinner. I tossed a rock of frozen hamburger into the microwave and punched enough buttons to launch the space shuttle. Nothing happened.

"No! You can't do this to me!" I yelled, punching the sequence again in case I wasn't speaking coherent micro-ese in my first attempt. Zippo, no zappo.

Emily bopped through the kitchen on her way to work at the local ice cream store. "See ya at eight," she said.

"Don't you want some dinner?"

"I'll eat something at work."

Chalk up one serving from the dairy, fat, and sugar food groups.

The clock said Mark would be home in fifteen minutes. I hoped he wouldn't mind ravioli with meat sauce à la iceberg. I leaned against the counter and closed my eyes.

"Whatcha doing, Mom?" Laurel asked.

"I'm trying to remember how I cooked hamburger before the invention of the microwave."

"How 'bout the stove?" she suggested.

Cocky kid.

I pulled myself out of my catatonic state and followed her suggestion, browning the frozen hamburger in one pan while water boiled for the ravioli in another.

The doorbell rang. Another lawn service wanted to take care of us. *Was that a hint?*

That's when it happened. That's when the ravioli boiled over.

And that's when I realized this particular independent woman couldn't do it alone.

I removed the pan from the burner and shut off every appliance in the kitchen, hoping to prevent further mutiny. I escaped. To the bathroom. I locked myself in. Voluntary exile.

"Mom?" Laurel said, tapping on the door. "Are you all right?"

I took a deep breath and held back a primal scream.

"I will be," I said.

She left me alone. But I wasn't alone.

It's not a noble position, sitting on the toilet seat next to a sink that needs scrubbing, a mirror that needs shining, and a used Kleenex next to, but not in, the wastebasket nearby. But God didn't mind since he finally had me where he wanted me—ready to listen.

"God, it's too much!"

I didn't hear a celestial voice echoing off the faucet. I didn't experience a flash of light as God granted me his revelation. God's voice came from within and was as comforting as a hug.

"It's about time you came to me," he said.

That's when I gave my worries to God. I relinquished the pesky cat and the freshly fertilized philodendron. I gave him Laurel's forgetfulness, Carson's arm, and Emily's junk food dinner. I asked him to take care of the weedy lawn and the pasta-encrusted stove. And I asked if he had any good ideas for dinner—now late and getting later.

And he answered. Not with words. With feelings. Serenity. Peace. Everything *would* be all right.

I transferred the Kleenex from the floor to the wastebasket, reentered the world and pulled out a phone book. I ordered pizza—with extra cheese. God approves of pepperoni.

God's way is so simple. Maybe that's why this independent woman didn't see it sooner.

Worry ties you down. Prayer sets you free.

The Best-Laid Plans

I thank Christ Jesus our Lord, who has given me strength, that he considered me faithful, appointing me to his service.

1 TIMOTHY 1:12

Sometimes we're so busy planning our futures that we don't appreciate the present....

I opened the envelope. And the winner was ... I scanned the letter, zoning in on the fateful words "We are sorry" or "We are pleased."

Mark raised an expectant eye over the top of his newspaper.

"I got a yes!" I said. "They're going to publish the article." I jumped out of my chair. "Gather up the troops, we're going out to dinner!"

"Again?"

My hands found my hips. "You know it's a tradition. Every time I get something accepted, we go out to celebrate."

He shrugged. "At last count, I think we were negative twenty-three bucks."

He was right. With a family of five, it was easy to literally "eat up" my earnings in the corresponding celebration dinner.

I grabbed my shoes and sat to put them on. "It takes time, Mark. When I get a book published we'll have plenty to celebrate."

"If," he said.

"When," I said, tying my second shoe with a stubborn flourish. "I've got it all planned out. Any day now a publisher will beg to publish my book. They'll pay me a ridiculous amount of money, and I'll go on a book tour where thousands of people will wait in the freezing rain for me to sign my book, and I'll be on *Oprah* and *David Letterman* and—"

Mark put a hand on my forehead. "Brain fever. It will pass."

I gave him my best pout. "It *will* happen, you know."

"Maybe."

"It will."

He pulled me to standing. "It's not up to you."

"But—"

"This may be all there is," he said (being much, much too logical). "Be happy with it."

I let out a sigh.

"You get your coat," he said. "I'll get the kids."

I sank back, my bubble suitably burst.

"It has to happen," I told myself. "It simply has to."

Trust the Lord with all your heart ...

"God wouldn't let me get my hopes up if my dreams weren't going to become reality."

Lean not on your own understanding...

"I work so hard. I try not to get discouraged. I try to be patient."

In all your ways acknowledge him ...

"If only I knew what the future would bring."

And he will make your paths straight.

I heard yelps from upstairs as Mark told the kids we were going out to celebrate the acceptance of another article. Whoops of joy.

Where were my whoops of joy? I'd just sold a piece of my work and yet I was acting as if it wasn't good enough. Instead of reveling in the wonder of the moment, I was dreaming of the unknowns in the future. The unknowns that might never be …

"Congratulations, Mom!" Laurel said, as she burst in the room. She wrapped her arms around my neck and gave me a kiss.

"Yeah," Carson said. "Congratulations to Mom and congratulations to us. We get to go out to dinner!"

"I like it when Mom gets a yes," Emily said. "Maybe she'll get one tomorrow and we can go out to eat again, and again, and—"

I ignored this reflection on my marginal cooking skills. "One day at a time, kids. Who knows what will happen tomorrow?" The scene in front of me seemed to brighten, as if a heavenly spotlight accented our living room. Warmth. Security. Family. I stooped to help Laurel negotiate a stubborn zipper. "Right now I plan to appreciate what I have."

"I plan to appreciate chicken fingers and French fries," Laurel said, pulling me toward the door.

It was a good plan—a plan for the moment. As for the future? I'd take it one moment at a time. The way God had it planned.

A Cup of Faith

For even the Son of Man did not come to be served, but to serve, and to give his life as a ransom for many.

MARK 10:45

I pulled into traffic. The smell of the burger and fries rising from the sack sitting on the passenger seat made my growling stomach roar. I resisted the urge to sneak a couple of fries. I knew myself too well. Once the salty potatoes touched my taste buds, the entire bag would be at risk. I retrieved the straw and rolled the top of the sack closed. A meager lock against my hunger, but it would have to do. In five minutes I would be home.

Traffic idled at a stoplight. I peeled the straw and poked it through the lid of my drink. I would reward my willpower with a sip. As I lifted the cup, I noticed something odd. I held the drink against the sunlight. The liquid stopped two inches from the top of the cup. I jiggled the cup gently, as if expecting the clinking of the ice cubes to prove me wrong. Nothing changed.

I'd been gypped. How dare they short my drink. *A person deserves to get what she paid for.*

I whipped my head side to side, gauging the possibilities of turning around, racing back to the restaurant, and telling them just what I thought of businesses that didn't give customers their money's worth. Fortunately (for me and the restaurant) I was boxed in by traffic. My only alternative was to abandon my car and bodily storm back across the roller coaster of trunks and hoods. I resigned myself to never receiving my rightful two sips of pop.

The light turned green. I turned the corner toward home. I took a defiant drink of my soda, thinking of the two sips that would never be mine. My jaw jutted forward as I wallowed in the inequities of life. *It wasn't fair.*

I needed some pouting music. I flipped on the radio.

" ...behold his hands and side. Rich wounds, yet visible above, in beauty glorified."

Uh-oh. My chin sagged in shame.

Talk about unfair. Jesus was blameless and yet he had endured—

Fumbling, I surrendered the drink to the cup holder.

"All hail Redeemer, hail! For Thou hast died for me: Thy praise shall never, never fail, throughout eternity."

What right did I have to complain about anything? Jesus had suffered the ultimate act of unfairness. Without complaint.

For me.

"Forgive me, Lord," I said to the One who deserved to get what he paid for. The One who often received a cup of faith that was two sips short.

Waiting for Grandma

I wait for the Lord, my soul waits,
and in his word I put my hope.
My soul waits for the Lord
more than watchmen wait for the morning.

PSALM 130:5-6

I came to know Grandma Ruth at her funeral.

Her passing was not a surprise. Not because she'd been sick, but because of her age: ninety-five. She was ill a total of twenty-four hours before she died. "Sign me up," my husband said.

She was an asset to the retirement home where she lived the last two years of her life, playing additional bingo cards for the "old folks" who didn't feel up to it (their prize? bananas). She never lost the ability to hear a whispered word from forty paces—whether you wanted her to hear or not. She was a voracious reader and merciless at canasta.

At her funeral in Minnesota, sitting in the pews of the Lutheran church she attended, I remembered Sundays, few and far between, when we'd traveled the eight hours to join her in worship. The filigreed oak above the altar, the old-fashioned hymn board announcing the songs of the day. Now the church was full—a vivid testament to a woman who had lived in the same community for nearly a century. As memories were exchanged I realized how little I knew of her.

My Grandma Ruth was born in 1900, the youngest of nine children of Swedish immigrants. As with most families at the turn of the century, happiness and sorrow were close neighbors.

She never went to school past the eighth grade because her mother was in ill health (having nine children had a tendency to be hard on a woman). As a consolation, her father gave Grandma an upright piano.

She married Grandpa in 1920, and tackled the toilsome life of a farm wife. No running water or electricity for many years. Daily meals of chicken, homemade bread, and pies carried out to the farm hands in the fields. Three children. A depression and a world war.

They moved into town in 1950 to the ranch-style house I grew to know as Grandpa and Grandma's. We'd gather there at Christmas where we'd be awakened at 4:00 A.M. by Grandma making coffee bread with candied fruit. There was the inevitable stair-step picture of the grandchildren (as the youngest, I was at the low end until I caught up—and surpassed—a few of my cousins). How safe we felt walking downtown to the Ben Franklin store where we'd spend our Christmas money on paint-by-number kits and Slo-poke suckers.

Grandma was independent enough to live without her beloved George for her last fourteen years. She grew prize-winning roses. The coffeepot was always on. Her copper-bottomed pots and pans were disgustingly shiny, and the smell of Ivory dish soap will always conjure up thoughts of her kitchen.

That's what I knew about Grandma. Until her funeral.

The pastor stood at the pulpit, making us laugh and cry as he remembered Ruth. Then came the story that would forever color my thoughts of her.

Just a few weeks before Grandma's death, the pastor had been at the retirement home visiting some of the residents. He found Grandma in the activity room, sitting alone. He sat next to her and took her hand. "How are you today, Ruth?" he asked.

Grandma smiled a knowing smile. "I'm waiting," she said.

She wasn't referring to the next activity.

She was ready to meet God and was patiently and graciously waiting to be called. No doubt, he would greet her at the gates of heaven with open arms and an angel chorus. Grandpa would be there too, waiting for his "Wifey."

I was not the only one who cried fresh tears at the story. I'd known Grandma had a deep faith, but I'd never realized how at ease she was with our God. How I wished I could talk to her again, to share this new knowledge. Ask her questions. How much I could have learned from her.

How much I *did* learn from her with those two little words—I'm waiting. The biggest tribute I can pay her now is to grow in my life until I, too, can say those words with a smile.

I'm waiting. *I'm waiting for you to save me, God.*